GOD – I'VE GOT CANCER

GOD – I'VE GOT CANCER

A message of hope for anyone
who becomes seriously ill

Dr Richard Scott

Terra Nova Publications

First published in Great Britain in 2013 by
Terra Nova Publications International Ltd
PO Box 2400 Bradford on Avon BA15 2YN

ISBN 978-0-9570473-6-5

Printed by Createspace
and in Great Britain by Imprint Digital, Exeter

Contents

To those I have known with cancer,
whose battles have led them to a better place

ACKNOWLEDGMENTS

Many people have contributed to this book. Some allowed me to publish fragments of their life stories; in doing so, they illuminated and softened the early chapters and for this I am grateful. Others, in their role as publishers, equally generously allowed me to refer to passages from their books, often with a piece of encouragement attached. Without them, the book also would not have come to pass. Finally, I would like to thank those whose constructive criticisms enabled me to shape the book, getting the right balance between academic content and hope.

I would also mention my deep gratitude to our work secretaries, Chris and Tracy, and practice manager Rachel, for all their help with the manuscripts. And a special mention to all my girls at home – Heather, Jess, Grace and Abbie – for their wonderful love, concern and support throughout my illness.

"For the one thing that everyone knows about cancer is that it kills. There is no curing the cancer patient: the most that can be hoped for is a temporary remission while the appeal court argues about the precise date of execution."[1]

PREFACE

As described in my book *Christians in the Firing Line* (Wilberforce Publications, 2013), in the summer of 2010 a sequence of events occurred which led to a hearing before the General Medical Council. This became a fight for the right to discuss faith at work. So began a two-year battle to clear my name.

Halfway through this ordeal came another unexpected blow: I developed bowel cancer. "Bad luck" a second time? I don't think so. All human beings have an enemy who especially detests Christians and who has undoubtedly tried to take me out. But this time he had shot himself in the foot. For whilst each event clearly has had its downsides, unexpected blessings have cropped up – blessings for me personally and I hope for others who have had the misfortune to become seriously ill.

This book is about those blessings. Blessings which are available and which have been proven to improve the health of individuals. If you are unaware of what I am talking about you stand in the majority. Only the events of the last two years have led me to investigate what I now know is beyond doubt: that whilst standard Western medicine successfully treats many diseases, there is another influence on illness which is profound and yet under-recognised. His name is God.

INTRODUCTION

NOT MY PLAN

Cancer wasn't part of my plan for the tail end of 2011. I had always been an active sportsman and placed a premium on being towards the top end of my age group in terms of capability and fitness. When I was three years old, my nursery teacher wrote that my physical development was progressing nicely. Kind of her, although it didn't say much for my mental progress which clearly lagged some way behind! Nevertheless, as I progressed through school and university hockey teams to play football for an East African village, and then returned to run the London Marathon, physical incapacitation was far from my mind. It is true that for any ageing sportsman muscular and arthritic niggles raise their ugly heads from time to time, but nothing that rest, physiotherapy and arthroscopic surgery couldn't deal with. Till now.

Cancer is something that happens to other people. Statistically it is risky, and like other doctors I am on the alert for symptoms and signs in my patients which may signal bad news. When suspicions arise, the NHS in the UK is generally magnificent in allowing specialists to be seen within a fortnight, with diagnosis and treatment usually not delayed. As a primary care physician I continue to support and prescribe for the patient, but only ever as an educated outsider looking in. Patients are ill, the clue is in the title; doctors are meant to stay well. But I haven't, and although some of my patients have been shocked to discover that their doctor isn't immune from illness, the truth is that none of us is – and this includes cancer.

Albert Schweitzer gave up a selfish life at the age of thirty to look after lepers. On contracting the disease himself, he raised a great cheer in the colony when he spoke of "we lepers". In writing this book, I am no longer an outsider looking in, but an insider looking out. And the view depends on where you are coming from. My background is both medical and Christian. As a GP-evangelist who has "prescribed" Jesus to many hundreds of patients in thousands of consultations, I already knew that God changes for the better the lives of those who follow Him. Then, recently, I came across statistics which actually prove that God is good for your health. And that is pretty handy when you are ill yourself.

But I haven't written this book for my benefit. Currently, there are approximately 14 million people living with cancer in the USA and the UK alone. For many, the diagnosis is like a death sentence. Inside is an enemy seemingly determined to get us, and our lives become like a seesaw as the disease does its best to pull us down, with the doctors opposing it hauling us back to level ground. Whichever proves the stronger we may imagine will determine whether we live or die and it is quite possible to become fatalistic in observing the battle played out in our lives. But in this struggle between good and bad, are we merely passive and acquiescent, simply taking what comes our way, or can we influence the outcome? What role might our minds play in confronting this evil, and is there a spiritual dimension to the disease? In other words, where does God come in?

INTRODUCTION

In writing this book, I started with a considerable advantage. I knew God was active in other diseases and logic dictated that cancer should be no different. But, as any scientist knows, hypothesis and logic alone are not enough. Proof is required. So began a mission to discover whether faith in God makes a difference in cancer.

PART ONE

"The knowledge that I have cancer never goes away. I am aware that I am dying every moment of every day, and every waking moment of every night. Each day is new territory for me...." [2]

In this first section of the book we will examine the statistics about cancer and uncover what has been discovered concerning God's impact on diseases. Unashamedly, I have begun each chapter with a Bible passage that illustrates the problem faced by those with serious illness. While the specifics differ from those of the present day, the issues and the solutions are essentially the same, allowing us to learn from what was written many years ago. That is helpful because we need real wisdom in confronting the evil ahead, and to meet it head on from a position of strength.

To begin, let's get to grips with the enemy and why it seems to be on the increase.

Chapter One

THE ENEMY IS RAMPANT

Whenever the Israelites planted their crops, the Midianites, Amalekites and other eastern peoples invaded the country. They camped on the land and ruined the crops all the way to Gaza and did not spare a living thing for Israel, neither sheep nor cattle nor donkeys. They came up with their livestock and their tents like swarms of locusts. It was impossible to count the men and their camels; they invaded the land to ravage it. Midian so impoverished the Israelites that they cried out to the Lord for help.[3]

When I was six, my parents took us off to Turkey for a year. I remember a few details only from that time in the sixties, including my father speaking Turkish with locals as he changed money, and my parents skiing down the high street in winter. In bed at night, the only book I can recall my mother reading to me was a thick, glossy *Illustrated Children's Bible*. I'm not sure to this day exactly why she did so for she remains agnostic, but I vividly recall the pictures and stories which had an effect years later on my teenage life.

One thing that stood out even in such an abbreviated Bible was that the stories were not sanitised. A child, Joash, rescued to become king after all his brothers had been slaughtered – why would that be included if a sugar-coated version of the truth was being presented? And God's people, the Israelites, always seemed to be at war with surrounding tribes like the Philistines. The narratives and the wonderful illustrations fascinated me, and not just because they were all that was available in those days. Looking back, it was because they were simply better and more true than any other book I came across as a child. Gideon's life was a fine example.

The Israelites were having a terrible time. Leaving Egypt, they had entered the Promised Land, only to disobey God's precise instructions on not mixing with the locals. Instead of displacing them, the foolish people bought into the local culture and paid the price in terms of God's favour. Now, severely weakened in comparison to surrounding tribes, their harvests were raided and their animals regularly taken or destroyed. The situation became so desperate that finally they came to their senses and cried out to the Lord for help. In response, He sent an angel to a poor man called Gideon, who was found timidly threshing wheat using a winepress, so scared was he of enemy discovery. Transformed into a mighty warrior, Gideon would defeat theMidianite enemy, and the nation of Israel would be restored once more.

The Israelites' massive problems were of their own making. One disaster followed another until there appeared to be no way forward prior to God stepping in. Modern life, too, can be overwhelming. As a family doctor working in a poor seaside town in Kent, I am party to life stories in which one nightmare is laid on top of existing awfulness. Unlike repainting a wall, where a new colour obliterates the old, every new problem simply adds to what already exists and vies for attention until, in desperation, a doctor becomes involved and tries to disentangle what has been built up over many years. One of my wife's patients is a good example.

Derek* rebelled against his parents at an early age and got in with the wrong crowd. By 14, he was already taking heroin and dependent on prescription drugs but didn't always take them as prescribed, overdosing in his early twenties. An emergency appendicectomy followed as an isolated incident, but the advent of Type 1 diabetes requiring insulin meant that daily injections were legally now part of his life. Illegal drug taking continued, however, and he first entered prison after being caught selling Ecstasy, aged 21. In his late twenties depression set in and he took the deliberate decision to omit insulin from his daily regime. As a result, he was admitted to hospital with a potentially fatal complication – diabetic ketoacidosis.

In his early thirties, continuing IV drug use led to the development of Hepatitis C. Liver disease had now added to his problems which included being single, unemployed and dependent on Diazepam and other medicines designed to alleviate the side effects of a life of illicit drugs. Living in bed and breakfast accommodation didn't help, and severe back pain added to the cerebral atrophy (loss of brain tissue) found on an MRI scan. Becoming suicidal, he was more depressed than ever and his situation was becoming critical.

When we first met him he had a girlfriend, Isobel, and, soon after, there was a small child called Penny. They accepted an invitation to attend church and welcomed a daily meal from the attached community centre. Heartbreak would still follow as they would lose Penny following a child protection conference, but their determination to get her back led Derek to stop taking heroin. Access to Penny was granted

but Derek's life was still far from settled. A lifetime of heroin and Methadone had damaged his teeth to the point that he needed a dental clearance and his diabetic control remained poor. A fractured thoracic spine in 2009 led to morphine medication, while sleeping, anxiety and finances continued to remain big issues. But, encouraged by his obvious improvement, Social Services agreed to return Penny to the family unit which was further boosted by the arrival of a second daughter. Both children and Isobel were subsequently baptised in their new church. Derek had planned to join them, but the time wasn't quite right. Nevertheless, he plans to be next in line.

Whatever age and environment people are born into, life usually finds a way of being tough. The Israelites' big issue was widespread poverty and fear due to marauding enemy tribes. In much of the world today, sadly, not much has changed, but in the West our problems tend to be more complicated and multi-layered. Like Derek, we may have had difficulties related to lifestyle, relationships, money or chronic ill-health. And even if none of these apply and our lives have been progressing swimmingly, the chances are that the business of normal life will still have occupied us fully. No need, thank you, for anything extra but we find ourselves over-ruled as cancer emerges and insinuates itself into our lives.

We may think of it as a relatively recent disease, perhaps a bit older than AIDS but much younger, say, than the plague, but in fact growths from what we now know to be cancer have been recognised throughout the course of human history. So why has cancer recently become such a big issue worldwide? Is it just a question of fear, because the disease still kills when other ailments are more treatable? Or is it because this fear is now being positively channelled into fun runs and other charitable activities raising money for research? Perhaps it is stimulated, too, by the profusion of so-called "miracle cures" which suggest that clearly something still needs to be done. But I think something else has placed cancer firmly in today's limelight: the public suspect that for all the progress made, the disease remains on the increase and what used to be widespread is now almost ubiquitous. And they are right – the enemy is rampant – and the reason is that we are living longer.

Life expectancy is soaring. When I was a boy in the 1960s, the average Briton lived into their early seventies. Now, Joe and Joan Average can expect another six years of life, and had they been born today they would have had an 11% chance of reaching a century. Working lives are being extended as a result, but one thing hasn't changed. The decision to continue working has always been profoundly influenced by the health of an individual. Most people put good health before work and money in terms of happiness, and certainly we are in better shape than our forefathers as we smoke less and exercise and diet more. Consequently, fewer of us are entering our graves as a result of heart disease, traditionally far and away the biggest killer in the Western world. Mortality from other causes is also down which is good news, but there is one disease which is on the rise: cancer.

Cancer isn't just a human problem. It is widespread throughout the plant kingdom, being seen in clover, sunflowers and other common plants. Animals aren't let off the hook either, with breast cancer common in dogs, and melanoma of the anus seen particularly in grey horses. Cattle suffer from tumours of the eyelids, whilst mice are afflicted with a variety of cancers, which explains their popularity in cancer research.[4]

Moving on to humans, although cancer has been observed throughout the whole history of medicine, knowledge about the disease was limited until the advent of the light microscope in the 17th and 18th centuries. But it took until the 19th century to learn that cancer cells differed from normal cells by having lost certain characteristics of their parents, becoming less recognisable and more embryonic in type, and that they also grew uncontrollably and spread, causing death if not restrained. Many causes for this cellular change have been identified but there is one factor which outweighs all others: age.

AN AGEING PROBLEM

The incidence of most cancers increases with age. Children who develop cancer under the age of 14 are certainly most unfortunate, with less than 1,500 cancers occurring annually in this age group in the UK and just over 11,000 in the USA.[5] Only 1 in 500 children will develop cancer, and teenagers and young adults below 25 are similarly well protected with only slightly more cases in this age group than in the youngsters. But while just over 1% of all cancers are seen in the first quarter century of life, as we grow older, the numbers begin to stack up, with 25 – 49 year old adults supplying 10% of new cases. Big trouble though arises in late middle age (50–75 years). Now cancer really begins to take its toll, with more than half of all UK malignancies presenting in this group, with the remaining third coming to light in the very elderly who are statistically the most at risk from the disease. Doing the maths, a whopping 89% of all UK malignancies come to light after 50th birthdays are done and dusted; and if we shift the goalposts slightly, in the USA the picture is similar, with more than three-quarters of cancers emerging after a person is 55. Cancer truly gets going as we grow older.

Why? The reason is simple: as we age, our cells correspondingly age and become more liable to cancerous change. So living longer will increase the incidence of cancer, just as the general public has suspected. And the rise has been dramatic. In the UK in 1975 there were 185,000 new cases. Twenty years later, the figure had reached 260,000, and by 2010, 317,000 new cases were recorded. In the USA, new cases in 2011 were expected to exceed 1.5 million, up from 1.2 million in 1999. Large figures, but still small in comparison to our increasing populations. But if one considers an individual's lifetime risk of developing a malignancy, the numbers really hit home.

In the late seventies, one in three Britons could expect to develop cancer in their lifetime. But two decades later the rise in cancer incidence had outstripped that of population growth so that the lifetime risk of developing a malignancy in the UK is now 42%, placing the UK in 22nd place overall worldwide. In the USA, a similar proportion (more than 2:5) prevails, but with men dominating the picture. A male in the USA currently has an near 1 in 2 lifetime chance of developing invasive cancer; American women, by comparison, are rather better off, but still more than 1 in 3 will contract the disease.

The trend is forecast to continue. It seems quite possible that in the not too distant future, the UK overall may follow the male trend in the USA with half the population developing a malignancy during their span on earth. My dictionary accords 'rampancy' the following attributes: unrestrained, violent behaviour or unchecked growth. Cancer fits the bill on all counts.

The family names have been changed at Derek's request.

Chapter Two

THE BIG BOYS

A champion named Goliath, who was from Gath, came out of the Philistine camp. He was over nine feet tall.[6]
At approximately 1,000 BC, the future King David was merely a shepherd-boy in a nation at war with their bitter enemies, the Philistines. On one famous occasion, the two sides gathered, each on a hill, with a valley between them. The Philistines' main man stood up and challenged the opposition to provide him with a single opponent. The result of their one-to-one battle would determine which nation would become the other's subject. The opportunity was significant, but the taunt was obvious: no-one would dare take on the giant, for Scripture notes that (King) Saul and all the Israelites were dismayed and terrified.

The story of how David alone was prepared to confront the defiant Goliath and rid Israel of disgrace is well-known, not least for the manner in which he accomplished his ends. Eschewing armour, he used only weapons familiar to him, a sling and a small stone, before success allowed him to cut off the Philistine's head. Their champion gone, his compatriots ran for their lives. The battle was won, but not by traditional means.

At over nine feet, Goliath remains the tallest man on record to date. His weight wasn't recorded, but fully clad in armour and described by Saul as a fighting man since his youth, he would have represented the greatest individual obstacle to any soldier alive then. Furthermore, his nation was the major issue that David's people faced.

The analogy with cancer is clear. Individually, it may well represent the biggest challenge that any of us will face. And nationally and globally, cancer is a massive problem. In 2008 there were an estimated 12.7 million cases of cancer diagnosed worldwide, and as the world population continues to grow and age, the trend is expected to continue. By 2030, 21.4 million new cancer cases per annum are predicted.

The Medical Journal of Australia reported that individual GPs will look after an average of 16 patients with a diagnosed cancer and will see an average of 4 new cases per year, amounting to 120 cases over a 30-year working lifespan. In addition, each GP must keep alert in preventing cancer and in managing suspicious symptoms, lesions and concerns.

It seems that the disease is quite out of control. But "cancer" is an umbrella term including many different beasts amongst its number. My intention is not to look at every individual malignancy for this isn't a medical textbook. Instead, I will concentrate on just three cancers in each sex which disproportionately raise their heads in Western populations. The big boys.

In the UK and USA, approximately one quarter of all tumours in men occur in the prostate, beating lung cancer into second place, just ahead of colorectal (bowel) cancer in third. Together they comprise more than half of all malignancies on both sides of the pond. In women, more than half of all cancers equally arise in just three organs. Breast cancer is far out in the lead with 3 in 10 cancers appearing in this organ, far out-ranking lung and bowel cancers in second and third places. Thus four cancers in total dominate the picture in the West.

But the situation is fluid. Cancer doesn't stand still, and despite the overall increase in incidence, some tumours are in decline.

TRENDS

For example, lung cancer in men, stomach cancer in both sexes and ovarian and cervical cancer are significantly reducing in frequency. Great news, but sadly other tumours are on the rise.

Malignant melanoma is the fastest increasing cancer in men and the second fastest in women. With thyroid cancer in women and liver cancer in both sexes also rising, the picture would appear bleak, were it not for the fact that such increases are not inevitable, as many of these cancers are preventable: melanoma relies on sun exposure, while many cases of primary liver cancer are linked to alcohol and illicit drug excess. Equally, while PSA testing has contributed to increased diagnosis of prostatic cancer, it also allows it to be caught much earlier, with better outcomes.

ANY RACIAL DIFFERENCES?

Cancer around the world is rising but the pattern of disease differs from that in the West. It is not therefore too surprising to discover that some of these ethnic differences persist on both sides of the Atlantic. In the UK, black and minority ethnic groups do much better generally than their white counterparts, being 20–60% less likely to develop malignancy. But there are some hiccups. Prostate, stomach, liver and cervical tumours are all more common in black people, along with myeloma.

In the USA, Hispanic women are relatively protected from

breast cancer, but along with Asians and some other recent immigrant populations, are more susceptible to cancers linked to infectious agents (stomach, liver and cervix), reflecting higher prevalence of infection in their countries of origin. Ashkenazi Jewish women have a genetically increased risk of breast and ovarian cancer, whilst African Americans again have an increased risk of prostate cancer but also aggressive breast tumours in their women.

TOSS OF A COIN

Currently, 42% of the UK population and an even higher proportion of American men will develop cancer at some point during their lives. As this figure rises and approaches the 50% mark, our chance of becoming a cancer patient is akin to tossing a coin. But does that mean that nearly half of all those living in the West today need fear dying from the disease? What proportion of those who develop cancer actually perish as a result, and is there any comfort to be found in the trends? How is treatment faring, and is standard Western medicine the only hope?

Chapter Three

WHAT ARE MY CHANCES?

*The L*ORD *said to Satan, "Very well, then, he is in your hands; but you must spare his life."* Job's second test.[7]

Job is a supremely interesting book. The angels line up before God for inspection. Among their number was Satan, the fallen angel, who had been roaming throughout the earth. His motives in doing so were well-known to the Lord and to prove the futility of his actions, God suggested that Satan consider His servant Job, knowing that this chosen man would resist the very great evil that would come his way. The challenge was accepted, but Satan was aware that there were limits to his malign influence over his victim. In effect, the evil one was kept on a leash – allowed to cause so much harm but no more. Whatever he got up to, the deal was he must not take Job's life.

Satan gave it his best shot, but failed to break God's man. Emerging from his onslaught, Job was even more blessed by God than he had been prior to his time of testing. Vast numbers of animals came his way, along with a new family of ten children. The Bible notes that, *Nowhere in all the land were there found women as beautiful as Job's daughters, and their father granted them an inheritance along with their brothers.* That's good, but for Job himself there was yet another favour to be enjoyed. After this, he lived a hundred and forty years; he saw his children and their children to the fourth generation. *And so he died, old and full of years.*[8]

We would take that, wouldn't we? Prosperity and a good long life, allowing us to see our children and grandchildren grow up? But the price paid to achieve it was high. It involved the most awful examination of his body and character; an examination he had never asked for but which came his way relentlessly as layer after layer of suffering poured down on him until he could just about take no more. Not knowing why this was happening and with no indication of how long his ordeal would go on, on more than one occasion he saw death as his only escape. But his suffering did come to an end and the latter part of his life would prove more than satisfactory. But only because he survived.

Survival. The big one. Most of us are prepared to go through tough times involving unpleasant treatment simply because we hope to live longer as a result. We may not even mind too much about developing cancer, because we know the disease is common and that common things occur commonly. What does matter is getting through to the other end alive and well, and that's something we'd quite like to know right from the beginning. So, in the manner of my Labrador pleading for food, we look up at our cancer specialists wide-eyed and ask, "What are my chances?"

It was a question I asked my oncologist. If I hadn't had any treatment, what would be my chances of being here in five years' time? What about if I'd just gone for surgery and kicked the rest into touch? What would the numbers say then? And now I've taken your advice with the chemo, how much extra life should that give me? Tapping my details into his computer, the answers emerged and helped me understand the science behind the decisions my wife and I faced in the next chapter. For the present, though, I'd like to concentrate on a young mum with aggressive breast cancer, whose initial numbers were grim and whose chances of survival would very much depend on her decisions concerning treatment.

Hilary is a 31 year old lady in otherwise perfect health who discovered a breast lump on self-examination. Catching it early, or so she thought, the tumour was less than two centimetres in size at diagnosis but was already Grade 3. At surgery, a single lymph node was discovered, after which she asked her oncologist what her chances were. "If you have nothing else done, Hilary, your chance of being alive in ten years is only 66%. Radiotherapy is necessary to reduce your risk of local recurrence but will have no influence on your survival. Because the tumour is quite aggressive, I recommend you have 3rd generation chemotherapy, which will reduce your chance of recurrence by a further 16.5%. Sadly, the cancer was both oestrogen-receptor (ER) and Herceptin (HER) negative and thus these avenues of treatment are not available to you. Had they been, your prospect of being alive in a decade would have increased by another 5-6%."[9]

Hilary asked the question and got her answer. Leaving aside the 7% or so of cancers where the primary is unknown and thus information is inadequate, most of us can also statistically assess our chances of survival. As individuals, this data is crucial in planning for the future. But as more of us are getting cancer, we need to grasp the bigger picture. Mankind's battle against the disease is gaining speed and treatments are improving, but how successful are we in keeping people alive? Is the fight going well or does more cancer inevitably mean more deaths from the disease? More questions means more facts are required, but again we have the data.

Cancer is the biggest premature killer in the UK and the second biggest in the USA. In 2009, it was responsible for 156,090 deaths in the UK – 69,000 more than died from heart disease and 109,000 more than from stroke. With 309,189 cases diagnosed the previous year, the death rate is approximately half the incidence rate, but whilst men and women are diagnosed in very equal numbers, more men die from the disease than women. The huge burden it places on society is probably best viewed in terms of percentage loss. In the period 2007–9, cancer caused more than 1:4 (28%) of all deaths in the UK, with just a slightly lower percentage expected to die from the disease in the USA in 2011.

If we look at death caused by individual tumours, again the not so fab four stand out. But the lung has surged to top the list, causing just under a quarter of all cancer fatalities in the UK and more than a quarter in the USA. The most commonly occurring cancers – breast and prostate – are consigned to second place, with bowel taking up the rear in third. Altogether the top three cancers account for nearly half of all UK cancer deaths with exactly the same percentage (47%) applying to American men, but the top three account for fully 50% of all cancer deaths in American women.

TRENDS

The good news is that death rates from cancer are coming down. Screening, earlier presentation, rapid diagnosis and better treatments have forced the mortality rate to plummet, with death rates reduced over the past 20 years by 22% in men and 14% in women, amounting to 900,000 lives saved in the USA during this period. Four of the five big killers – male lung, female breast, prostate, and bowel in both sexes – have all been affected, with only female lung cancer bucking the trend, reflecting more recent smoking habits.

Some of the less common killers have seen even greater falls, with death from stomach cancer down by a third and cervical cancer by 30% in the UK. Nevertheless, some particular challenges remain; death from liver cancer is up by a third on both sides of the Atlantic, while more UK women are dying from uterine cancer and men from malignant melanoma than a decade ago. Furthermore, little improvement has been achieved in reducing deaths from leukaemia, ovarian and pancreatic cancer and there is another area of concern. Seven percent of UK cancer deaths are of unknown origin. Until accurate diagnosis is possible, these deaths will be hard to stem.

LIVING WITH CANCER
Self-evidently, as cancer becomes more frequent but death rates fall, more of our populations are living with the disease. Exactly how many people this applies to is hard to quantify precisely, but the number of people who have been diagnosed yet remain alive at a given point is definitely on the up. Some will have been cured; others not. Prevalence thus reflects both the incidence of cancer and survival from the disease.

For example, in 2007-8 it was estimated that just over two million people in the UK and 11.7 million in America were living with or beyond cancer. More than two-thirds will survive five years and over a half will survive beyond a decade. Taking into account both the rise in incidence and that in survival, the prevalence of the disease in the UK is predicted to rise by a not inconsiderable 3% every year. Living with cancer will therefore become even more common than it is now, especially in two of the most common cancers: prostate and breast, where the outcome is relatively good. But there is one factor which mitigates against survival with cancer.

THE ROLE OF EDUCATION

Whilst all will applaud the fabulous work done in reducing death rates from cancer, a sense of disquiet remains. Considerable disparities had long been recognised between the haves and have-nots in the USA particularly, with those of low socioeconomic status considerably disadvantaged with respect to dying from cancer. And the gap is growing.

In 1993, the least educated black and white men in America had a cancer death rate already double that of their more educated peers. By 2007, the difference had risen to nearly three-fold. What's responsible? Certainly, unhealthy lifestyles involving inadequate diet and exercise, with excess smoking, play a part, but discrimination in health care added to health insurance issues means that poorer Americans tend to present later with more advanced disease. Whilst genetic and cultural factors shouldn't be ignored, Dr. Samuel Broder, then Director of the National Cancer Institute, stated in 1989 that "poverty is a carcinogen". We should rightly hail the USA for progress in reducing fatalities from cancer, but much work remains in minority and otherwise poorer subgroups if the overall picture is not to be further skewed towards those less fortunate in American society.[10]

WHAT ELSE IS POSSIBLE?

Before I leave the maths alone, one thing must be made plain. Death rates are falling, but the huge increase in incidence still means that each year more people will die from the disease. What can be done about this?

Obviously, an enormous amount of work and expense is already dedicated to prevention, diagnosis and treatment. But is there anything else which is proven to improve prognosis? I am not referring here to the wonderful Macmillan nurses in the UK and others who tirelessly work to improve a cancer patient's lot. They are already part of the system and play a vital role in relieving suffering. Nor am I thinking of the myriad of alternative treatments available, many of which have been offered to me in the early days of my disease. Aromatherapy, scalp and hand massage and even Reiki are currently available on the NHS in the UK. These techniques may well be pleasurable, but they cannot claim to be anything other than palliative without proving their case. But there is one approach to dealing with cancer which does have a strong evidence base and yet of which many remain unaware.

Chapter Four

A DIFFERENT APPROACH

Now there is in Jerusalem near the Sheep Gate a pool, which in Aramaic is called Bethesda and which is surrounded by five covered colonnades. Here a great number of disabled people used to lie – the blind, the lame, the paralysed.... One who was there had been an invalid for thirty-eight years. When Jesus saw him lying there and learned that he had been in this condition for a long time, he asked him, "Do you want to get well."

"Sir," the invalid replied, "I have no-one to help me into the pool when the water is stirred. While I am trying to get in, someone else goes down ahead of me."

Then Jesus said to him, "Get up! Pick up your mat and walk." At once the man was cured; he picked up his mat and walked.[11]

The pool at Bethesda was supposed to have curative powers. In some manuscripts, an extra verse was added which explained the prevailing view that an angel would stir up the waters on occasion and that only the first into the pool after such a disturbance would be healed. This poor invalid obviously subscribed to this belief but lacked the means to take advantage of where he was. We don't know how many others were healed in the years that he lay there, but his frustration was obvious. With no-one to assist him, how could his situation ever change, and even when Jesus showed compassion on him, he probably viewed the stranger simply as a pair of arms to help him get to where he needed to be.

One of the strangest aspects of this story is the man's ignorance of who Jesus was. Elsewhere, the severely disabled and leprous actively sought him out, so desperate were they for healing. But this man seemed completely unaware of who was in front of him. Blind to new possibilities, his focus remained on what he thought was his only hope – getting into the pool – despite it having availed him little so far, and he might have remained an invalid for the rest of his life had Jesus not taken charge of the situation and offered him healing. But that wasn't the end of the story. This man now had a decision to make, the most important of his life. Would he continue to trust purely in what he was used to, hoping against hope that the familiar would come up trumps, or would he realise that something extraordinary was on offer and grasp it with both hands?

Get up! Pick up your mat and walk. The instruction was clear and so was the challenge to his preconceptions. Up to now, he had assumed that his future was purely dependent on others. Without them, he had no chance. But Jesus was saying something different. Where convention dictated that he was a passive spectator unable to influence his own healing, Jesus gave him an active role to play. Picking up his bed and walking wasn't simply a matter of the poor man obeying a command. Instead, it involved him turning his back on the past and looking forward to a future with the Lord who had made him well.

Long ago, this man was given a new start in life. After 38 years, we may feel the poor beggar deserved a break and we are glad that things worked out well for him. But in a sense, so what? 2,000 years ago and 2,000 miles away from the UK and further still from the USA, how, we may ask, is this relevant to us today? He was an invalid and we have cancer and Jesus isn't exactly wandering around the West nowadays in person, dispensing healing like sweeties from a jar. It's a nice story but let's get real – even if he was there, doing stuff, we're here and what happened then doesn't take place now. And to be frank, there's quite enough to do fighting cancer without fairy tales distracting us from the business in hand. So let's leave Jesus out of it and stick to what we know, trusting in our doctors to heal us as best they can. But what if such a view proves detrimental to our health? That in denying Jesus, we deny ourselves the very help that only he can give?

A woman from New Mexico had been diagnosed with chronic leukaemia by a doctor in Albuquerque. Attending one of Benny Hinn's monthly crusades in Tulsa, Oklahoma, she was healed, with papers later confirming that she was free from blood cancer. Another woman, this time from Las Vegas, watched one of Hinn's daily TV programmes in which clips from the healing crusades were shown. Cured by simply watching the programme, her doctor said that this was the first time he had ever seen such a thing and her insurance company even dropped her rates when the healing was confirmed![12]

For those without faith, this must sound very odd. Cancers healed through prayer or by watching the TV? Really? Granted, if it's true it's well worth having, but there will be those who need a whole load more convincing before they are prepared to sign up to a God who heals today. I think that's a reasonable position to hold, so before I make any more big statements, it's only fair if I explain precisely what has led me to conclude that supernatural healing is possible and that there is hope beyond standard Western medical treatments for those who are sick. To do so, please indulge me as I lay before you my illness and another recent crisis which threatened to derail all I had worked for, but which have cemented my belief in a God who not only heals, but who has a good plan for the lives of all in His Creation.

TWO CRISES AND A BOOK

I noticed a change in bowel habit and an irritating passage of slime, but kept it to myself, ignoring the inner voice to do something about it. Doctors aren't always smart when treating themselves, and certainly any middle-aged patient coming my way with similar symptoms would find themselves rapidly becoming acquainted with a colonoscope. Bleeding eventually forced my hand and as the scope entered my tail, I very rapidly came face to face with a nasty looking polyp. Surprisingly, the biopsies came back benign, but a subsequent wide removal of the growth under general anaesthetic confirmed the unpleasant nature of the beast, a moderately differentiated adenocarcinoma of the rectum. And it wasn't alone – scans had already confirmed there was a large lymph node keeping it company.

Back home, it was no great surprise when the extensive raw area bled heavily post-op. Naturally, no-one else was in the house at the time, so with one hand holding a pad to my nether regions and the other mopping drips from the floor and packing a bag for hospital, multi-tasking reached new heights as I persuaded 999 not to delay the ambulance. Cautery under a second anaesthetic stopped the bleeding and a few days later I again returned home. After a few unsuccessful attempts at peeing, I finally managed to get rid of the catheter (readers who are men will appreciate this fine moment), allowing me to progress to chemo and pelvic radiotherapy lasting five weeks.

Recovery this time went more smoothly, give or take a little incontinence, and further scans thankfully came back clear. To be honest, I would have been pretty disappointed otherwise, rather presuming that the lymph node would get clobbered by the radiation coming its way; but to learn from the oncologist that only one in five people in my situation actually achieve radiological clearance somewhat increased my gratitude, not least because it helped my wife Heather and myself decide what to do next.

For some with cancer, the treatment path is clear. Once the diagnosis is made, an algorithm (standard procedure path) kicks in: treatment A leads to treatments B and C, with scans and other tests checking on progress along the way. But for others the situation is not always so straightforward, and the patient is faced with at least one tricky, momentous and potentially life-changing decision.

The surgeon had successfully removed my cancerous polyp, but now recommended that the rest of the rectum should follow. Major surgery in bowel cancer has always been integral to "gold-standard" treatment, as it gives the patient the very best chance of avoiding local recurrence in the future, a situation I am naturally keen to avoid. But the times they are a-changing; studies are increasingly showing that for selected patients with low rectal tumours, chemotherapy alone may be the way forward. This avoids the permanent side effects of major pelvic surgery whilst mopping up any misbehaving cells not detected by scanning but lurking elsewhere in my body. Chemo was a given, but leaving the organ in place where the problem arose is cutting edge medicine. With my life on the line, to operate or not to operate, that was the question.

By now, I had already chatted to a second, more senior,

surgeon who was distinctly less keen for me to undergo the knife. Equally, whilst my local oncologist felt obliged to reiterate that surgery remained standard procedure, a London Professor of Oncology, in reviewing my case, said that if I was his brother, he would watch and wait. Different opinions, but what to do?

Now a doctor is no different from any other patient when it comes to family and friends giving advice. A medical colleague said if he was in my position, he would have everything done. An old friend from medical school who had just recovered from extensive reconstructive surgery following breast cancer, gave the same advice. But another professional, this time a barrister, whilst fully admitting his ignorance of matters medical, threw in his two-pennyworth that dignity was important and that a colostomy wasn't worth it. Most of the rest adopted a middle position: seeing my dilemma, they ventured no opinion but agreed to pray for the right decision.

For this, more than any well-meaning advice, Heather and I were thankful. Life involves so many decisions. Some are minor, others more significant. This was massive. Get it wrong by choosing surgery and I faced a lifetime of pelvic complications, with still no definite promise of being clear from cancer in the future. Get it wrong by not choosing surgery and I would kick myself if the tumour recurred locally, leading to more extensive surgery and a potentially bad end. It is no exaggeration to say that we really needed to get it right!

From the beginning, even before radio and chemo, we always knew that this would be the moment of truth. A decision would have to be made, one way or the other, a decision which would affect my entire future. Throughout the months of pondering what to do, one thing was paramount. I had to know what, or whom, to trust. I started by ruling myself out; not only had my body emphatically let me down, but I had compounded this fallibility by bad decision-making, resulting in delayed presentation. With me out of the way, why not rely on the system? Certainly, the medical technicians batting on my side have been absolutely first-rate and I am confident that they will continue to do their best for me. But their attempts to thwart the adverse intentions of the third biggest malignant killer in the UK and the USA remain at the mercy of statistics. Please don't get me wrong here. I have nothing but admiration for those in my profession and the system in general, but for me it is not enough. So where do I choose to turn at this moment of crisis, and why?

To begin, I must firstly mention a second crisis which preceded and overlapped my health predicament. Over the last fifteen years, my work as a Christian GP in Margate has been enlivened by reaching out to the many drug and alcohol addicts and those otherwise at a low ebb who appear endemic in our seaside town. Spurred on by seeing some stunningly awful lives change as a result of the gospel, it has been relatively easy to take firmly on the chin any complaints from those not overly delighted to receive such an approach from their doctor. However, a complaint was made about my having referred to matters of Christian faith in the course of a consultation. To learn how I got on with my professional body (the GMC) and for details of other UK Christians being marginalised at work, please consult a book I have written on behalf of Christian Concern, entitled *Christians in the Firing Line*. (Wilberforce, London, 2013)

My reputation as well as my life under threat, I needed help and got it from two London-based organisations: Christian Concern (lawyers) and the Christian Medical Fellowship (CMF). The legal team defended my name, but the medics' contribution would be no less significant.

For some time I had been aware that studies have shown that practising the Christian faith has considerable health benefits. These studies simply confirmed what I already suspected from my own experience, but in today's audit society, statistical proof is increasingly needed to convince sceptics that God not only exists but remains very active in the lives of His people today. By directing me to the relevant literature on spirituality and health, the CMF not only opened my eyes to the sheer volume of work on the subject, but to a central truth: God is indeed good for your health. That's handy when you are trying to convince disbelieving lawyers of your intentions in bringing God into a medical consulting room; it is also no bad thing when serious illness strikes unexpectedly.

SCIENCE AND RELIGION ARE COMPATIBLE

The first scientific attempt to examine the effect of religion on health was somewhat laughable. Galton, a half-cousin of Charles Darwin, took the very reasonable view that all matters of human importance should be subject to investigation. He was particularly interested in whether prayer worked; if it did, he reasoned, more prayerful people should live longer than those who prayed less. But he foundered early on; assuming that religious ministers were likely to be highly prayerful and that the Royal family would be the recipients of many prayers ("God save the Queen"), his discovery that ministers barely outlived doctors and lawyers, and that members of royal houses actually had lower life expectancies, caused him to conclude that no statistical evidence existed for the efficacy of prayer! Clearly, he had not taken into account either religious martyrdom or the danger inherent in high office in those days, but at least he had made a start.

We should be grateful to Galton, for his original point

was well made: if religion is related to survival, then science ought to be able to detect its effects. And many years later, somewhat gallingly for him, it has been found that despite many fervently religious people sacrificing their lives for their faith, clergy from a variety of faith backgrounds (both Protestant and Catholic) and cultures (Western and non-Western) do indeed experience a lower risk of early death.

Science has progressed a long way since Victorian times. But it was not until 2001 that three professors, Koenig, McCullough and Larson, looked comprehensively at the evidence pertaining to religion and health. Initially ridiculed by epidemiological colleagues who viewed their investigations as a waste of time, they discovered score upon score of studies on the health effects of religiousness which no-one seemed to care about. In total, they examined over 1,200 research studies and 400 reviews from around the world, covering the period from the 1800s to the year 2000. All papers included had been assessed as scientifically reliable and valid, and the result was a massive tome, a *Handbook of Religion and Health*, indisputably the seminal work on the subject.[13] Since then, a second edition (2012) has been released,[14] owing to the exponential increase in research since the millennium in this new field of religion, spirituality and health.

As they examined the research, Koenig and his fellow researchers found that the great majority of papers came from America and that they pertained predominantly to the Judaeo-Christian tradition. They did discover papers from other countries and other faiths, but overwhelmingly the evidence applied to the influence of Christianity on health in America. As the findings were shown to be similar in other countries, I feel it reasonable to generalise the findings to the UK too. And the results were dramatic. As a taster, here are a few stats from the first edition.

81% of all the studies showed that religious belief was beneficial to health. By contrast, only 4% showed evidence of harm. For example, a 1987 study showed that church membership reduced mortality in the middle-aged. This was backed up by another report ten years later which followed a 28-year study in 5,000 people. Startlingly, religious attendance more than once a week led to a 36% reduction in mortality, which was highly significant even after adjusting for healthy living. But the largest study to date is my personal favourite. 21,000 American adults were observed for 8 years; regular church attendance led to 7 years longer life expectancy, and 14 years if black!

So religious membership and especially attendance seem to be beneficial. What about private religious activity? Does that also lead to longer life expectancy? In a 1995 study of 232 patients undergoing elective cardiac surgery, those who did not draw on religion for comfort or strength had a three times greater mortality. Put another way and even more strikingly, those who drew on religion and had social support had a mortality rate fourteen times lower! A six-year study on 3,800 healthy adults from North Carolina again confirmed this: those who didn't pray or study the Bible again had a higher death rate. Not every study was positive, but an overall meta-analysis of data from more than 125,000 subjects confirmed that religious involvement is substantially and significantly linked with increased survival.

My interest in numbers and statistics has already been betrayed in previous chapters; as medicine is becoming less idiosyncratic and more evidence-based, such an extraordinary bias towards health improvement should be of great interest to government bodies, as well as giving hope to individuals. My appetite was whetted, but I wanted to know more. In particular, if religion improves survival overall, does its protective effect apply only to certain specific diseases or more generally to all illnesses? And does faith in God mainly help diseases of the mind, or does it also protect the body from a wide range of physical illnesses? For this is a book about cancer, in which the mental effects are considerable but where physical damage actually kills. I needed Koenig to give me a detailed breakdown and he didn't disappoint.

Chapter Five

IS FAITH GOOD FOR MENTAL HEALTH?

Do not be anxious about anything, but in everything, by prayer and petition, with thanksgiving, present your requests to God. And the peace of God, which transcends all understanding, will guard your hearts and your minds in Christ Jesus.[15]

Working in Margate since 1998 has been a real eye-opener. Previously, I had been a junior surgeon and worked at various levels in Accident and Emergency in the UK, sandwiched between which were spells as a missionary doctor in India and in Tanzania. So I entered general practice with a relatively wide background in medicine, but now came across issues that I had hardly encountered in depth previously. Many drug addicts congregate in seaside towns in the UK; Heather and I would discover that one of the main reasons we had been led here was to help this segment of the local population. And one symptom which comes up time and again in drug addiction is anxiety.

Recently, a patient from the drug scene phoned me. Denied access to his son, he was terribly upset and understandably anxious about when they would next meet. Stuttering more than usual, he was barely able to speak and we needed to meet in person so that I could help him with his fears. But anxiety is not restricted to substance abusers. Indeed, it appears to be almost endemic in our area, with young men commonly suffering from chest pains due to tension and the middle-aged often stressed and anxious about their jobs. An elderly lady springs to mind too. Family fall-out had taken place over her late partner's will and she would see me regularly, tearful and very shaken about the future.

Whilst anxiety appears to be on the increase, it is clearly not a new symptom. The apostle Paul tackles the subject in his letter to the Philippians and his teaching is tough. ***Do not be anxious about anything*** is a bold statement and one that we might superficially resent. Clearly, he has no idea what we are going through and just how hard our lives are. If he had, he would never have penned those words. Yet Paul wrote this letter from prison. Many in his position were facing execution, and his life was one of repeated beatings and escape from danger. He had plenty to worry about but chose not to, arguing that a better way forward is to give everything to God and let Him deal with it. After all, if Jesus died on the Cross because of all the rubbish in our lives, surely that would include anxiety, which is not only troublesome but highly unproductive. Give it to Him, Paul says, and you will be left only with peace.

Whilst anxiety presents in my surgery almost as frequently as depression, another all too common complaint also caught me unawares. A patient turns up a little sheepish. Badgered to contact the doctor, he admits that anger has got the better of him and that verbal violence on occasion may turn physical. Relationships dear to him are under threat, and given an ultimatum by his spouse or one last chance at work, he begs for help. The moment is critical in his life or her life, as Amanda amply demonstrates.

Amanda first recalls becoming angry aged three, when her father was thrown out of the house by her grandmother. She was never to see him again. Her mother remarried when she was five and her father was deleted from her memory until she was fifteen, when she discovered that her stepfather wasn't her real dad. A few days later, the first incident took place. Her parents were having an argument, and as her stepfather moved towards her mother, Amanda spun round and kicked him through the conservatory window. Recovering in ICU for several days, he made a full recovery and police charges against her were dropped. On two further occasions, arguments with her led to him being knocked out and hospitalised through a deft kick to the chin, before she was moved out of the family home and went to live with her grandparents.

Once Amanda's powerful build and martial art skills led her into trouble at the dentist. Warned that she normally needed two injections to provide the normal level of anaesthesia, his reassurance that one should do the job led her to thump him when it didn't! Needless to say, she was not welcome there again and doctors, too, were not immune from her ire.

The first anger management specialist she went to see was laid out by her within weeks. Of the five subsequent doctors she saw in this area, two would also receive severe physical ill-treatment when her dark side took over. Benefitting little, she called it a day and moved to Kent with her partner, Jim. Joining our surgery, she spotted a poster advertising the next Alpha Course and the two of them not only joined the course but gave their lives to God on it. As new believers, they chose to take part in several future courses to learn more and in order to help others.

Amanda admits that anger still raises its ugly head from time to time, but I quote: "Now whenever I feel anger I start to pray there and then; after, I always feel like I'm floating on air for a few minutes, then I begin to cry. The anger goes and the frustration is released through my tears." She goes on to say, "For those of you who have a problem believing this, I challenge you to spend some time with me and find out for yourselves. Let me warn you of this first: I'm a second Dan black belt in Taekwondo and a purple two sash in Wing Chun Ku-Foo! Leaving that aside, she concludes, "All you have to do is believe. It will be the hardest thing you've ever done, but the best. Becoming a Christian, life is hard but full of amazing experiences. God bless."

Addiction, anxiety, depression and anger - all part of a GP's normal lot, and if we add in bitterness, lack of forgiveness and an inability to love through never having been loved, it is obvious that medics can be presented with massive challenges at work. What we do at this point really matters. Some patients will respond to simply chatting through issues with their doctor. Others need the help of counsellors, psychologists and psychiatrists. Many require medication in the short and long-term but by no means all are helped by these standard Western approaches, with anger counselling particularly impotent in my experience to change lives. The question is: why?

Many doctors would argue that we cannot be expected to sort out all our patients' problems and that we can only give them what we have to offer. In saying that, they absolutely hit the nail on the head. For whilst pills and professionals can be very helpful, the conventional mental and physical model is limited, and if that is all we have to offer, we will miss the mark on many occasions. All of these symptoms tend to be linked to bad life experiences, and whilst counselling may bring these to light and modern potions may dampen them down, to really move forward patients need to replace these recurring bad memories with something so good that it transforms their lives. Harmed by evil actions, whether their own or others', all have ailments with a spiritual element, and spiritual illnesses need spiritual solutions. This is where God, the author of all things good comes in.

Amanda discovered that only God could deal with her anger. But a single individual cannot prove that God makes a difference to others. I needed to know whether God is involved in more than just the occasional case of mental illness and to a degree that was not only powerful but could be statistically proven; so I turned to Koenig for answers.

In the 2001 first edition of his handbook, a considerable proportion of the 1,600 papers and reviews concerned mental health. 79% found that religion led to greater happiness and better morale. A study from Michigan showed that self-worth was lowest where there was very little religious commitment. Church attendance also led to greater life satisfaction, whilst belief in the supernatural and miraculous disposed 81% of people to be optimistic concerning the future and to have more purpose and meaning in life.

So religion seems to be generally good for a person's well-being, but does it help with specific conditions? With anxiety becoming so widespread, this would seem a good place to start but correlation isn't straightforward as anxiety may lead people to turn to religion. However, half of the papers since the year 2000 have shown that anxiety is reduced with religion, with only 10% showing a definite increase in anxiety with faith. Religious intervention also improved anxiety in most studies.

What about depression? Overall, 61% of 500 studies show that the more religious were not only less likely to get depressed but also to stay depressed as they recover up to 70% faster if depression does set in. Social factors are partly behind this.

Almost all studies show that religion leads to better social support and thus the religious tend to be less lonely and adapt better to bereavement. They also have more stable marriages in nearly nine-tenths of research to date.

That's fine and dandy, but much of what has been stated so far might have been predicted. Although those suffering from depression, loneliness, stress, anxiety and poor self-esteem would almost certainly not agree, sceptics might consider these conditions as "softer" and thus most amenable to religious intervention. But what about more serious mental illness? Surely religion wouldn't be of much use here?

Work in schizophrenia suggests otherwise. Out of 10 studies, definite benefit was noted in four and no harm resulted from five, while in the last study something rather imaginative took place. Twenty schizophrenics received weekly prayer and Scripture reading from student nurses. All demonstrated notable improvements in mental state and functioning as a result. Since then, more work has been done with psychoses, although it is fair to say that the picture isn't straightforward as many psychotic patients will report religious experiences as part of their condition. Nevertheless, the religious did report less psychotic symptoms overall than the non-religious, and following religious intervention, rehospitalisation of psychotic patients was reduced in two-thirds of the studies.

What about drugs and alcohol? Having worked with so many addicts over the years, I was particularly keen to know whether my personal experience of the Christian faith reducing consumption in at least some patients would be replicated by Koenig's findings. Gratifyingly, more than 85% of 250 studies showed a reduction in alcohol usage with religious input and the effect on drug abuse was no less impressive with 86% less drug abuse among the religious. His conclusion that excess alcohol consumption and illicit drug use are highly susceptible to improvement with religion is borne out in the life of one of our patients.

Tyrone mastered certain skills early in life. Posted through windows from the age of nine, he would open doors for his brothers to ransack and steal. Given by his mother into the care of Catholic nuns as she couldn't control the "hyperactive little bleeder", he ran away repeatedly, often sleeping in houses he had broken into. Falling through a roof after stealing its lead, he first did a spell in a detention centre then entered borstal and prison, which merely improved his physical fitness whilst teaching him new ways to make money.

Ty first tried heroin aged twenty-three. Thieving three times daily to fund his habit led to further custodial sentences, and by the time he had had enough of London and came to live with his mother in Margate in 2002, he had spent 17 of his 42 years in prison. Attending our GP practice, he received treatment for drug abuse and was encouraged to come to church but still continued to offend. Attending an Alpha Course in a suit after his brother's funeral, he was teased by a younger alcoholic lad and offered to sort out their differences outside. Highly combustible, he was kicked out of his home by his mother and sensed his life falling apart.

Further prison sentences led to him getting on well with a particular chaplain, and he began to read the Bible. Then his cell neighbour hung himself, and Tyrone's drug taking increased, both in and out of prison. Discharged in 2004, he began to sleep rough, and I recall a memorable night when he turned up at church soaked to the skin and wearing two left shoes! The curate and I took him to an overnight hostel but he was arrested after failing to return the keys. By now pneumonia was setting in and his physical condition was becoming critical. Despite being very weak in prison, with his weight down to eight stone, he was still considered to be so dangerous that he was handcuffed continuously to policemen.

Eventually, four litres of pus was drained from his left chest, and as he slowly recovered, walking the hospital corridors with his minders, he came across the chapel. It took three days for a security pass, but when it arrived, and still handcuffed, he knelt down and cried out to God for forgiveness, and thanked Him for saving his life. Suddenly, he felt warmth all around him, warmer than from any "gear" he had ever taken and a reassuring presence from Someone close that all would be OK. Vowing to have more faith in Jesus, the obvious change in him led him to being released from prison five months early.

Initially on the outside, his life took on the old pattern but then he remembered the chapel and knew that things would only turn for him through the church. He began to attend twice a week and felt the Lord say to him, "Enough is enough. If you need My help, I'm here. Please ask." In 2005, he gave his life to Jesus and was baptised, along with four other ex-addicts.

Since then, a life of stealing has been consigned to the past, whilst drug-taking is now rare. Ty has a new flat in Margate and is a keen semi-professional gardener. Best of all, his sister, Belinda, also gave up a life of heroin and was baptised after seeing the difference God had made in his life. A final word from the man himself: "Drugs are nice, but will kill you. Jesus is better and won't."

Tyrone and Belinda amply illustrate the massive social and financial implications of religion benefitting health; but there is more. Koenig's team wanted to know whether other types of antisocial behaviour could benefit from religion. They discovered that delinquency and crime were reduced in 78% of studies, but would also learn that another social disaster was not ignored by God.

Religion helps those who self-harm. Approximately 70% of studies show that it leads to less suicidal ideation and fewer attempts, whether successful or not. Put together, these results are striking. Religion (and notably the Christian faith as this was the spirituality applying to the vast majority of cases) seems to be good for mental health. Perhaps a last word should be reserved for an expert in the field. A former President of the Royal College of Psychiatrists was so taken by the strength of the evidence that he stated, *"for anything other than religion and spirituality, governments and health providers would be doing their utmost to promote it."*

Chapter Six

WHAT ABOUT PHYSICAL HEALTH?

In those days [King] Hezekiah became ill and was at the point of death. The prophet Isaiah son of Amoz went to him and said, "This is what the LORD says: Put your house in order, because you are going to die; you will not recover."

Hezekiah turned his face to the wall and prayed to the LORD, "Remember, O LORD, how I have walked before you faithfully and with wholehearted devotion and have done what is good in your eyes." And Hezekiah wept bitterly.

Before Isaiah had left the middle court, the word of the LORD came to him: "Go back and tell Hezekiah, the leader of my people, "This is what the LORD, the God of your father David, says: I have heard your prayer and seen your tears; I will heal you. On the third day from now you will go up to the temple of the LORD. I will add fifteen years to your life." [16]

I mentioned earlier my childhood delight in discovering the stories selected to be in the glossy *Illustrated Children's Bible*. Now as an adult, I am party to the real deal, the entire Bible, and the tales of the early kings do not disappoint. Warts and all, the monarchs essentially come in two types: those who did evil in the eyes of the Lord, following the detestable practices of the nations around them with idolatry topping the list, and those who did what was right in the eyes of the Lord. Hezekiah sat at the top of the second category: *Hezekiah trusted in the Lord, the God of Israel. There was no-one like him among all the kings of Judah, either before him or after him. He held fast to the Lord and did not cease to follow Him; he kept the commands the Lord had given Moses. And the Lord was with him; he was successful in whatever he undertook.*[17]

Hezekiah might have been a very good king but it didn't prevent him from getting ill. Right at the point of death, he receives a visit from the prophet Isaiah. This was almost certainly his last chance of being healed and I guess he was looking for some healing prayer, but instead received bad news: God has decreed that your time is up, so get your affairs in order. It was all over. In some respects the news was helpful as any uncertainty about the future had been taken away. Not only did he suspect he was dying but God had just confirmed it! But by no means was it the news he was looking for, and the hammer blow to his future ambitions must have been severe.

Hezekiah may have been king but he was first and foremost a God-fearing man. He had just received a death sentence, but that didn't stop him praying. He started by reminding the Lord of his faithful devotion to Him, but in his grief was unable to talk much and at this point simply wept. And the Bible records that the Lord was moved by what He saw. Having decided that Hezekiah would die, this is a clear example of God changing His mind in response to a request from His people. We then learn that Isaiah told him to prepare a poultice of figs, which was then applied to the boil and he recovered. The Lord healed him using a local remedy in this instance.

In the last chapter we looked at the evidence for God as a

"mental health provider" and found it to be convincing. But to learn of God physically healing a man close to death is even more encouraging as this is a book about cancer, where the physical effects ultimately predominate. If God is to play any role in the big one, logic suggests that all other physical diseases should be subject to His intervention. But, as ever, logic is not enough – the case must be proved. To discover whether "doing God" is good for our bodies as well as our minds, I needed to turn again to Koenig. But first, a case history from America.

John was a 35 year old gay man living in San Francisco. Complaining of feeling tired all the time, he was especially concerned because his partner had recently been diagnosed as being HIV-positive. Despite taking special precautions since the diagnosis he was scared and after a fortnight attended his doctor. A rapid test for HIV in the doctor's office was negative, but a formal blood test sent to an outside laboratory came back positive.

John was shocked and overwhelmed for he now had the dreaded disease from which so many of his friends had died. Despite the offer of medication, he knew what lay ahead. Although he had been brought up in church and remained a believer, John had not attended services or prayed regularly for years. The diagnosis, however, made him think more of religion and he knew of a church elsewhere in the city attended by many gay men. Better still, one of his closest friends was a regular attender and had been encouraging John to go with him.

Over the next two months, John became a regular churchgoer and began to pray privately again. Over the following years, this pattern continued and he

encouraged others, including his partner, to join him. But his partner wanted nothing to do with religion and, after a while, John got tired of asking. Five years down the line, his partner progressed to AIDS and three years later he died. John remains well ten years after he was diagnosed with HIV and has not yet developed AIDS.[18]

His life turned upside down, John turned back to God. Individually, his decision proved to be a good one, but if others are to be encouraged to follow his lead, clear evidence on a much grander scale that God is good for physical health is required. Whilst by no means all of the major diseases have been investigated thus far, there is now a considerable body of evidence that shows the positive influence of religion on physical health. Let's begin with the biggest killer in America.

CARDIOVASCULAR DISEASE
Cardiovascular disease (CVD) encompasses coronary heart disease, hypertension, peripheral vascular disease and stroke and affects nearly 80 million US citizens. In 2005, CVD claimed 865,000 lives (35% of all deaths), exceeding the combined fatalities from cancer, accidents, Alzheimers disease and HIV/AIDS. The biggest contributor by far is coronary heart disease.

CORONARY HEART DISEASE
Coronary heart disease (CHD) is responsible for nearly half a million US deaths a year due to heart attacks. If religion is to have any effect on physical disease, this would be a good place to start. Koenig began by looking at physical risk factors and found that religious belief and behaviour

reduced BP, cholesterol, alcohol consumption and smoking whilst improving diet and exercise taken. Furthermore, by reducing depression and stress whilst improving well-being and social support, it should also reduce the likelihood of CHD as these, too, are risk factors. Thus there are very good reasons for hypothesising that religion should have an effect on heart disease – now to prove it.

In 1973, an Israeli study on 10,000 Jewish men found that the more religious suffered fewer heart attacks over a three year period. This finding was confirmed a decade later, as secular male Jews had a heart attack rate four times greater in men and seven times higher in women than Orthodox Jews. The death rate was also affected.

The same was found to be true for Christians. In the 1960s, coronary heart disease was found to be significantly lower in "church-goers" than in "non-church-goers", a finding confirmed in 2008 following cardiac catheterisation studies. In the 1970s, frequent church attendance more than halved the risk of dying from CHD, while in 2006 heart attacks in men aged 60 or over were two-thirds less likely to occur in those regularly attending religious services, with death also reduced in this cohort by 40%. Even mortality following surgery is influenced by religion. In 1995, mortality following elective coronary artery bypass graft (CABG) surgery was much lower (5%) in even occasional church attenders compared to 12% in those who never attended, a finding confirmed by a more recent study from 2009. As ever, not all papers produced positive results, but those that didn't were very much in the minority.

Less coronary heart disease and fewer heart attacks with better results from surgery is impressive, but what about other cardiovascular diseases? In particular, does it influence the single commonest cardiovascular abnormality, high blood pressure?

HYPERTENSION

Hypertension (BP > 140/90) affects about 20% of adults in many countries and nearly 30% of the US population over the age of 18. It contributes to nearly half of all deaths in the USA through heart and peripheral vascular disease, stroke, renal failure and aneurysms. Even small improvements in hypertension reduce the health risk, and as fifty million Americans have raised BP and two million new cases are discovered annually, there is considerable interest in treating this common disease in ways which don't purely rely on medication. Should this include religion?

Sixteen studies have looked at religion and blood pressure. All but two found lower BP among the more religious, with diastolic BPs particularly reduced. One early exotic study from 1963 involved 1,000 Zulus in South Africa. Rural churchgoers and women in urban churches were less hypertensive, a finding which has been repeated in over 80% of American studies, especially amongst those who prayed frequently or who studied the Bible at least daily.

So religion is good for the heart, but what about for the brain? Work in relation to stroke and Alzheimer's disease is in its infancy, but thus far papers indicate that religious attendance does reduce the risk of stroke, helps patients cope with their illness and may reduce the physical disability resulting from attacks. Equally, half of the studies into dementia show better functioning or slower decline in cognitive functioning with religion, with only three finding otherwise. Early days, but less disability from stroke gives hope to the 48 million (22%) of Americans who live with all kinds of disabilities. Might religious involvement help the disabled cope with handicap or even prevent disability in the first place?

Virtually all early studies found that physical disability

was inversely related to church attendance. On the surface this might appear obvious, as decline in physical functioning would affect an individual's ability to get to church. But this reduction in attendance is usually only temporary as three years later those with severe handicap were again attending services. And it is well worth them doing so, for a 1997 study of 2,800 persons showed that those that attend have healthier lifestyles and less disability! Furthermore, those with higher levels of disability appear to benefit more from religious involvement than the less disabled, with their mental health also improving from attending. This mental improvement is particularly important, for not all will report physical improvement with religion. Don comes to mind.

"I am Don and I suffer with multiple sclerosis, an illness made more bearable by my Christian faith. I was diagnosed at the age of 38 but had known for years that my body was behaving badly. As a schoolboy I was picked to run cross country for Kent and had always been active but my body was no longer able to function so the diagnosis at least put a name to my disease. I attended an Alpha Course when I finally had to give up work and discovered the love and friendship that exists within the Christian Church.

"I discovered how despite my own illness and shortcomings I liked and enjoyed helping people with alcohol and drug dependency. A verse that I have always had in mind is Matthew 28:19–20 and I have found that by spreading the Word of God, lives can be changed and I got to see and feel the joy that enabling someone to discover Jesus brings. I know my illness is getting worse and miracles are supposed to happen but

instead of asking why me or why not me in the case of miracles, I get on with life and experience joy in all my experiences whether they be good or bad. You cannot experience pleasure without pain but at times I would like the quantities to be different."

Over the past two decades, Don's MS has slowly deteriorated. As his doctor and friend, this had been painful to watch and I cannot say whether his faith has helped slow his physical decline or not. But fifty studies in the past decade in the area of physical disability have shown promise here. Once more, religious attendance consistently predicted lower levels of disability and slower deterioration over time. Good news, but prevention would be even better. Posing the question whether religion might help to prevent disability in those who are already ill led to further work which suggested that it can. In 1995, patients recovering from heart transplantation functioned better post-op and had fewer health worries if religious, while another study found that of 30 women admitted for hip fracture surgery, those who were religious were able to walk further at hospital discharge. Again, not all studies were positive, although some of the negative studies examined "spirituality" rather than traditional religious attendance, weakening the analysis.

Finally, before we move on to cancer itself, does religion reduce pain? In 1986, some patients with chronic low back pain were divided into subgroups and the cohort which used prayer and hope as a coping strategy reported less pain. A 1973 study of 44 orthopaedic patients then discovered that those who received daily chaplain visits of fifteen minutes reported less pain and stress, needed less analgesia and took up less nursing time than those for whom it was business as usual. And the majority of papers from the last decade have also shown that religious interventions and activities reduce pain over time.

The subject is not straightforward however for, as with anxiety, religion maybe used as a coping mechanism by those in pain after other methods of pain relief have failed. Nevertheless, the majority of papers from the past decade also show that religious interventions and activities reduce pain over time. How nice if future work could determine whether the same applies to pain relief in other chronic conditions, e.g. chronic fatigue syndrome and fibromyalgia.

These findings are highly relevant, for in the next chapter I look at cancer, where pain can be such an issue. But as a taster, religion and pain were studied in 71 patients with advanced cancer in Vermont in 1981. The sample was highly religious, with over 90% believing in God, 80% feeling that prayer was helpful, and half that church was very important in their lives. All the indicators of religiousness measured, including belief and church attendance, led not only to well-being but to lower levels of pain. The authors concluded that closeness to God was inversely related to the presence and intensity of pain. Now for the big one....

Chapter Seven

AND CANCER?

Jesus looked at them and said, "With man, this is impossible, but with God all things are possible.[19]
Jesus had been approached by a rich young man. *"Teacher, what good thing must I do to get eternal life?"* A decent question and one which showed that whilst he clearly appreciated the finer things in this life, he still had one eye on the main event – eternity. Jesus enquired back whether he had kept the commandments and discovered that he had. But the young man correctly sensed that something was still missing and asked him, *"What do I still lack?"* At this point, Jesus must have looked into his heart and discerned his biggest problem. Telling him to give away his possessions and then follow him, his advice proved a step too far and the young man *went away sad, because he had great wealth.* His biggest problem was money – in this case too much of it – allowing Jesus then to give his famous teaching on a camel, the eye of a needle and a rich man attempting to enter the Kingdom of God.

At this juncture, the disciples were astonished and asked quite reasonably, *"Who then can be saved?"* They appreciated the extraordinary difficulty this pious young man (or ruler) faced in doing what their Master recommended. Given his circumstances, it seemed practically impossible for him to move beyond his present situation. Seeing their difficulty and no doubt knowing that others following them would be faced with seemingly insurmountable issues, Jesus provided what they (and we) needed to know: *"With man, this is impossible, but with God all things are possible."*

I find this a huge spiritual confidence boost. Our God is the God of the impossible. Were it not so, if He was just someone who made possibilities happen, He'd be no better than a good man who worked hard or simply got lucky. Instead, what we may regard as impossibilities, God sees as opportunities for action, should we believe and trust that He can do so.

A junior anaesthetist in the UK was asked to see an old man with intolerable pain due to metastatic carcinoma of the prostate affecting the spine. He inserted an epidural and started an anaesthetic infusion which relieved the immediate pain, allowing him to talk to the patient. It was night-time, the ward was quiet and the old man was heartbroken because he was estranged from his alcoholic daughter. Longing to be reconciled before he died, there seemed no likelihood and he also had another issue. Having neglected his God, he felt guilty about turning to Him now after ignoring Him for so long.

The anaesthetist asked him if he would forgive his daughter if she returned. Of course he would; the longing was obvious in his face. When asked if he thought God would forgive him too if he returned to Him, he burst into tears as the point hit home. After the epidural infusion was taken down, his pain did not recur and he was reconciled to his daughter, who was seen pushing him round the hospital in a wheelchair.[20]

The old man chose to return to God and what seemed

impossible took place in his life. Tragically, the young man in the Bible story – when faced with a similar choice – didn't. Clinging to what he was used to and knew was possible, he stuck by a life dominated by possessions which did not satisfy. Trusting Jesus to help him through the difficult transition to a new life, one in which he was materially poorer but spiritually richer, proved to be a step too far, even though it offered him the very thing that he desired – eternal life. By going for the easy option, he would never discover how God would have helped bring about the impossible in his life. Even having encountered Jesus the miracle worker, the God of the impossible, he still walked away sad with his biggest problem unresolved. But for those of us with cancer, his discussion with the Teacher can prove highly advantageous. We, too, have a big problem which dominates our thoughts. We, too, can approach Jesus for help and would love to see God do the impossible in our lives. But before we do, just in case you have forgotten, here's a quick reminder of the extent of the enemy.

As we saw earlier, cancer is the second biggest killer in the UK and USA after cardiovascular disease. Around a quarter of all dying in both countries do so from the disease, and on both sides of the Atlantic it is the biggest cause of premature death. In terms of absolute numbers, 300,000 people contract the disease every year in the UK, with half this number dying annually, whilst in America the comparative numbers are 1.5 million new cancer diagnoses and over half a million succumbing to the disease each year.

We know too that the numbers of people affected by the disease are increasing. In 1999, there were 3,300 new cases diagnosed a day in the United States, amounting to an annual incidence of 1.2 million.[21] But as death rates have fallen on both sides of the Atlantic, even though cancer still claims 450 UK and 1,500 US lives a day, present-day survivors now number more than two million in the UK and eleven million in the USA. So with a lifetime cancer risk greater than 2 in 5 on both sides of the Atlantic, the question must again be posed: in such a frightfully common and virulent disease, is there anything beyond standard Western prevention and treatment that might alleviate the chance of both getting cancer and dying from it?

Earlier, I reported Harold Koenig's findings on religion and heart disease. Firstly, he and his co-workers looked at the influence of religion on risk factors for the disease, then they turned their attention to whether there were better outcomes in the disease itself with religion. Adopting the same logic here, they needed firstly to identify risk factors for cancer before examining any possible religious influence. Many of these risk factors are psychosocial and little different from those playing a role in heart disease. Their mode of action is through impairing the body's immune system.

THE IMPORTANCE OF IMMUNITY

The immune system has many functions. It deals with outside invaders, particularly viruses and bacteria, but it also acts as the body's first line of defence against cancer by being constantly on the lookout for any malignant cells that spontaneously arise. If this inner enemy is spotted, the immune system gets going by directing several specialised cells to hunt down and destroy the unwelcome invaders. One of these special agents is the T lymphocyte which increases in number and morphs into natural killer (NK) T cells, whose job is to destroy tumour cells. The war is on, and one way to determine how well the body is doing in cancer is to measure the activity of these NK cells.[22]

For example, in 1987, a study of 75 women with Stage 1 or 2 breast cancer found that those patients with positive lymph nodes (spread of disease) had lower NK cell activity and correspondingly reduced survival compared with those with non-metastatic disease (no spread). Koenig now wanted to know whether psychosocial factors like stress and depression which were known to inhibit immunity, did so by influencing NK cell activity.

RISK FACTORS MAY BE CARCINOGENIC

Two early studies in breast cancer patients found that they did. Then in 1994 it was noted that women who were lonely, emotionally repressed or who had recently suffered a family bereavement were more likely to be diagnosed with a new breast cancer. Similarly, stress increased the chance of developing cervical tumours by 27%. Finally, in the year 2000, more than 6000 Jews who had lost an adult son to war or accident were found to have twice the risk of developing lymphatic or blood cancers and a higher chance still of malignant melanoma.

Stress also adversely affects the progression of cancer. By liberating cortisol, which binds to receptors on cancer cells and stimulates their proliferation, stress has been proven to lead to poorer survival in breast and prostatic cancer patients. But this alarming finding does bring with it some encouragement, for where stress can be reduced through psychosocial interventions, metastatic spread of the disease is limited, improving survival.

Depression also impedes immune function, with two American studies showing a doubled risk of developing cancer. Worse still, a report from Finland involving more than 7,000 adults over a 14 year period found their chance of developing lung cancer rose more than three times if they were depressed. Granted, cancer and depression can co-exist and depression tends to be high where cancer is advanced. But these findings emphasise that a vicious cycle can be set up in which depression and cancer stimulate each other, ending in premature mortality.

Anxiety also doubles the risk of dying from some cancers, whilst another Finnish study of 2,400 men over 6 years found that mortality from both cancer and heart disease was raised 2–3 times in those with moderate or high levels of hopelessness. By contrast, optimism has been found to reduce death from cancer whilst social support prolongs survival in breast cancer and malignant melanoma. So the way we respond to cancer is important.

Andrew is a Christian in his early 50s. Four years ago, he received unwelcome news. I quote: "A diagnosis of cancer is always a shock, and to be told at age 48 you have prostate cancer which if left untreated will be life-shortening turns your world upside-down. Things that you took for granted are now uncertain. Plans for the future may be irrelevant and amid this turmoil you have to discuss and plan treatment and surgery. Fears and worries crowd in, sleeping becomes difficult and everything gets out of perspective.

"At this point, my faith in a loving omnipotent God provided fixed reference points for restoring my perspective. God had proved trustworthy in difficult situations in the past; why would he suddenly abandon me now? Jesus Christ is the same yesterday, today and forever; so I could trust that God would be there whatever the future held. Above all, knowing that God loves Sandra my wife and our children, Fiona and Michael, more than I do, and that's a lot, gave tremendous peace of mind. Knowing that whatever happened, and even if I died, God would be there to support and guide their future lives reduced my anxiety.

"However, it's not just the big things where faith is

important; it is in the small practical day-to-day issues. Following surgery, I had to have daily radiotherapy. Parking at the hospital is notoriously difficult as spaces are limited and the surrounding streets are for residents only. I had to arrive on time for my radiotherapy sessions with a full bladder that was still recovering from surgery. Being able to park quickly and near to the radiotherapy department would make life far easier and less stressful. As a family and supported by friends and members of our church, we prayed that I would find a parking space. Every day that I had to have radiotherapy I found a parking space immediately close to the hospital entrance.

"You may feel this is just coincidence, but I agree with Archbishop William Temple who when he was mocked that "answered prayer was mere coincidence" replied, "That may be true, but I've noticed that when I pray coincidences happen and when I don't, they don't."

Andrew's existing faith helped him with worries which naturally arose when cancer raised its ugly head in his life. Choosing to trust in God at this juncture made a big difference to him and his family. But what if he hadn't had family backup, if he had been a single man with few friends and little social support? The evidence suggests that his chances of developing cancer and doing badly from it might have increased, and has inevitably led to researchers delving deeper. For example, is there such a thing as a "cancer-prone personality", for it looks like those who are emotionally repressed, angry or loners may have a greater chance of developing cancer than those with expressive personalities. Naturally, the point is made not to point the finger at personality types being responsible for their own disease or with a view to fatalistically suggesting that that is just the way it is. Instead, with psychological treatment already having improved outcomes for some with breast cancer, further work relating to personalities may provide another way forward in cancer.

So far, stress, depression and hopelessness have all been found to be carcinogenic and to worsen outcomes from the disease, whilst optimism and social support act to improve survival. The importance of all these findings is obvious when one considers how religion reduces risk factors and improves the positive influences at work. But again it is not enough for researchers to merely postulate a religious effect on cancer. Direct evidence is required.

CANCER AND RELIGION

As early as 1962, it was reported that patients with cancer of the rectum were less likely to be members of a religious body and attended services less often. Two later studies confirmed that the religious enjoy up to a 30% lower risk of colorectal cancer. Other cancers studied show a similar pattern. In 1966, regular attenders amongst 4,000 women in Washington had less than one-third the number of abnormal smears or confirmed cervical cancer compared with infrequent attenders, whilst a 1989 study of 3,000 adults showed that those who lived healthily and attended church weekly had an 87% lower risk of developing any cancer compared to the general population.

These papers were not alone in noting considerable risk-reduction with religion. A thirty-year study from the 1960s to the 1990s involving 6,500 people in California found that infrequent religious attenders were one-third more likely to develop cancer than at least weekly attenders. How can this be?

We already know that stress hormones are bad guys,

causing cancer to develop and progress, and that religion helps reverse this by helping people cope with anxiety, stress and depression. But more recently, a study from Italy revealed a further mechanism by which religion reduces cancer. Some patients were undergoing chemotherapy for metastatic lung cancer; those who had higher spirituality scores tended to have higher pre-treatment and post-treatment lymphocyte counts and as a result responded better to treatment and lived longer. Thus at least part of the positive effect of religion is likely to be through its effect on immunity. And that is important in countering the argument that religion only has an effect through encouraging healthier living.

NOT JUST BETTER BEHAVIOUR!
It is a fact that up to two-thirds of cancers are preventable. Cigarettes, excess alcohol, inadvisable sexual activity and sedentary behaviour can all be modified. All tend to be reduced when religion is taken seriously, with conservative Protestants having particularly low mortality rates at least partly for this reason. Healthy living is undoubtedly important, but before improvements are simply put down to this, two factors must be considered.

Firstly, such behaviour has stemmed from religious belief and commitment. Healthy living hasn't arisen *de novo*, it is a belief-based behaviour. Secondly, as we have already noted, religion impacts psychosocial factors which in turn influence the immune system, lowering the risk of cancer. And religion helps in another way. When cancer does intrude on life, faith proves helpful in coping with the crisis.

COPING WITH CANCER
Many studies confirm that religious beliefs and activities are commonly used by cancer patients. With their lives under

threat and out of control, sufferers are fearful and anxious about the disease, likely treatments and of course death itself. Some will turn to God for the first time; others, already faithful, pray with renewed vigour; common requests are for strength (for themselves and their families), for peace and for a cure. In addition, some of those for whom time is short will turn to Him in preparation for death and the afterlife.

For example, nearly 90% of breast and gynaecological cancer patients surveyed stated that religion helped them to cope with cancer and to sustain their hopes, with half of the gynae patients confirming that they had become more religious since having cancer. 17% even accorded their suffering some meaning as a result of their faith and none became less religious. Hospice patients in another report were less anxious if religious, while a 1995 study of lung cancer patients in Canada only put religion behind family as a source of support. Gross's remark that "when misery is the greatest, God is the closest" would appear to ring true.

Religion not only helps people cope subjectively with cancer, but objectively can be seen by others to be of help in the disease. For example, when 62 cancer outpatients were asked a single question: "Is God in control of your cancer?" those who felt He was were rated by nurses as having adjusted better to the disease.

Finally, religion has also been shown to help family members cope with that most awful of situations: cancer in a child. In-depth interviews with 118 affected families in 1991 showed that religion helped to protect and defend individuals, motivating them to cope constructively.

Many who would describe themselves as non-religious would accede to the idea that religion may provide some comfort in tough times. But far more controversial would be a statement that religion not only reduces the incidence of cancer but may even bring down the death rate from the dreaded disease. I can almost hear people say: go on – prove it.

SURVIVAL

The $64,000 dollar question is: do the faithful really survive cancer better? One early study in 1981 failed to show that they did, but involved only those with advanced cancer with only a one year follow-up. But the next year, a paper reported results from studying 1,800 men. Those who were inactive in church had a nearly seven times greater chance of dying from lung cancer than elders and priests. Then, in 1989, a study revealed that white non-smokers who attended religious services at least weekly were nearly 50% less likely to die from cancer, and more frequent attenders had a further 39% reduced chance of dying.

That is of interest, but to back up such a big statement more statistics are needed. And we got them in the 1990s, when data from the National Center for Health Statistics (covering 3,063 counties in America) dovetailed with information on church membership. It showed that religion, defined as that percentage of the population with full church membership and agreed religious conservativeness, was significantly and inversely related to cancer mortality. The Norwegians then reinforced what had been noted in America, backed this up, finding that the religious among 253 cancer patients were not only more satisfied and less hopeless but lived longer, experiencing a 15% lower chance of dying.

More recently, prospective (forward-looking) research followed African American women for 10 years. Those who developed breast cancer were 4 times more likely to die if they possessed no current religious affiliation. In fact, if they were not religious at all, their risk went up 10 times! And those expected to be the most religious of all, the religious professionals, confirmed this trend, enjoying up to 40% less lung, oesophageal and cervical cancer. Only the slightly increased risk of breast cancer in nuns bucked the trend and even this was expected as they don't enjoy the protection afforded by breast feeding.

In summary, there have been at least 28 studies looking at the relationship between religion and the risk of cancer developing and progressing up to death. Seventeen of these studies showed a definitely reduced risk, with only two reporting an increased risk. Statistically, it is therefore pretty clear that religion not only greatly reduces the risk factors for cancer, but also is proven to reduce cancer itself. Cancers are less common in the religious, and when the disease does occur, the outcomes seem to be better.

Long ago, Galton's proposition that religion should be subject to scientific investigation has spawned thousands of papers so far. But God's activity in health is hardly limited to that which has been formally studied. Anecdotal evidence since biblical times far exceeds that recorded by scientists. If there were just a few rare examples, one might justifiably be tempted to ignore these stories as quaint oddities, inconsistent with a God who generally doesn't intervene in the life of His people. But supernatural intervention by God in the form of healing miracles has been reported so often and in such numbers that they practically scream out for our attention. To my mind, the evidence is so great that simply putting one's head in the sand and stating either that God and miracles don't occur (atheism) or that the age of miracles is over (cessationism) are simply untenable when faced with the facts.

"Miracles. Really? Today? Are you sure?" For if God still heals supernaturally, right here, right now, any individual and family struggling with cancer would want to know more. OK, you asked for it....

Chapter Eight

MIRACULOUS HEALING

One day Peter and John were going up to the temple at the time of prayer – at three in the afternoon. Now a man crippled from birth was being carried to the temple gate called Beautiful, where he was put every day to beg from those going into the temple courts. When he saw Peter and John about to enter, he asked them for money. Peter looked straight at him, as did John. Then Peter said, "Look at us!" So the man gave them his attention, expecting to get something from them.

Then Peter said, "Silver and gold I do not have, but what I have I give you. In the name of Jesus Christ of Nazareth, walk." Taking him by the right hand, he helped him up, and instantly the man's feet and ankles became strong. He jumped to his feet and began to walk. Then he went with them into the temple courts, walking and jumping, and praising God. When all the people saw him walking and praising God, they recognised him as the same man who used to sit begging at the temple gate called Beautiful, and they were filled with wonder and amazement at what had happened to him. [23]

The crippled man knew where to beg, but on this day asked the wrong people for money. But instead of walking past him disdainfully, the two disciples demanded and got his attention. They had something far more valuable to offer and his healing not only delighted him but had an extraordinary effect on all those who knew him. Luke, the author of Acts, describes the people as being *filled with wonder and amazement at what had happened to him*; a miracle had taken place literally in front of their very eyes and I would wager he was not the only one praising God that day.

The Bible is full of healing miracles, both before and after the earthly ministry of Jesus. I do not intend to document these here, as there is a perfectly good book that one can consult for more detail! My particular interest lies in what God is doing in the here and now. Jesus told his followers that they would do even greater things than they had seen him doing, through faith in his name.[24] With no end point on earth attached to that statement, miraculous healing should have featured regularly throughout the last two millennia and continued up to the present day. The question is: does it?

Some might argue that with the advent of modern medicine the need for miraculous healing has diminished. Certainly, I would agree that all healing ultimately is from God and that He often uses medics to administer this gift. But there is a limit to man's ability to treat disease; we cannot cure everything coming our way, and thus the need for miracles remains. Indeed, miraculous healing not only continues but arguably is on the increase, and it's not just because improved communication makes us more aware of what is taking place in developing countries where first-world facilities are absent. Even close at hand in modern day America, supernatural events are being recorded in such numbers that it is increasingly hard to ignore anecdotal evidence concerning miraculous healing throughout the twentieth century and into the twenty-first.

For all of us alive today this matters. Even if currently we are fit and well, one day illness may strike. When it does, its effects may be acute and short-lasting or chronic and persistent, like cancer. Either way, we take the medical treatment offered, hoping that it will do the job, and on many occasions it does, with doctors able to improve the quality of our lives. But what if the limits of modern medicine are exceeded, if a disease proves resistant to treatment, or recurs? Or if statistically the numbers (and your chances) don't look too good. This is where an alternative approach comes in: prayer requesting God's miraculous touch.

Ever since my faith was reignited in my late thirties, older and wiser Christians have pointed me towards books providing example after example of God using his servants mightily as His instruments for healing in the past century. As I read of amazing faith and stunning results, I was always uplifted but never dreamt that one day I, too, might need His healing hand. But when I did, at least I knew where to look. So I offer you a few of these examples, a sample of what is possible through faith, beginning with the remarkable healing ministry of a Bradford plumber in the first half of the twentieth century.

SMITH WIGGLESWORTH

Wigglesworth was a remarkable man. Trained as a plumber, his healing ministry would later take him around the world. Laying hands on the sick, he would vigorously rebuke and cast out disease. A passionate advocate of divine healing, he wasn't against medical treatment, seeing doctors as having *"a work that no-one else in the world has to do ... a great suffering world of trials and sickness and sorrow."* Indeed, he personally took their advice, avoiding eggs after being informed that they might exacerbate his kidney condition. But he did take the view that doctors should only be paid if their patients were cured, preferring people to place their trust in God rather than purely in medical science.

Bold and audacious in his work, no disease seemed

beyond his faith for healing. On one occasion, a woman who had had 16 ear operations, including the removal of her eardrums, claimed she was so deaf she wouldn't hear a cannon go off. After anointing and prayer for the drums to be replaced, she heard a pin drop and began to preach. In Wellington, New Zealand, a deaf and dumb lady began to speak the name of Jesus, while a man with an imperfectly healed broken leg walked away confidently after the leg was rubbed and prayed for, leaving his crutches behind. Another time, a poor, twisted and deformed man approached him. After getting the whole assembly to pray, Wigglesworth told the man to drop his sticks, walk and then run. He did so, to the great joy of all present. And God can be even more creative.

He was staying with a clergyman who had no legs. After supper, he told the unfortunate man to buy a new pair of shoes in the morning. Thinking he was the victim of a cruel joke, the curate retired to bed, only to hear God tell him to "Do as my servant has said." Excited, he arrived before the shop opened the next morning but the shop assistant, looking at his artificial legs, felt it unlikely that he could help. Undeterred, the curate suggested black shoes, size 8. He then took off his artificial legs, and as he put one stump in the shoe, a leg and foot instantly formed. The same took place when the second shoe was tried on, and he left, wearing the shoes appropriately and with the staff gaping in astonishment.

With good humour, Wigglesworth would describe praying for individuals as "retail" healing, while mass prayer without contact he termed "wholesale" healing. He first employed this technique in Stockholm in 1921, when the police prevented him from laying hands on people. Another method he adopted for healing those he couldn't see in person involved praying over and anointing handkerchiefs with oil, in the manner of St. Paul in Acts chapter 19. Thousands around the world were healed remotely after receiving these handkerchiefs, including a man with appendicitis and his son with a large neck growth.

CANCERS HEALED

Wigglesworth had a particular dislike for cancer, regarding it as one of the worst diseases from the devil. At a service in San Francisco, he prayed for the sick, and a man with stomach cancer was brought to him on a trolley. After plunging his hands into the man's stomach, and causing the man's doctor to panic, the patient got off the trolley ten minutes later, praising God for his healing. A woman in Los Angeles, with cancer causing bleeding, was cured when the cancer was cursed, died and came out of her in a ball. A man with oral cancer spat it out after prayer, losing blood but healed of disease. In Northern Ireland he entered a room where there appeared to be no hope. A mother was dying from a tumour and the little girl alongside her was blind – both were healed. A particular favourite of mine, for obvious reasons, concerned a man with cancer of the rectum. In such agony that he required morphine injections every ten minutes throughout the day, he was prayed for in Jesus' name. During prayer, the cancer burst; the man's nurse didn't understand what had happened, but the patient knew God had done it.

THE DEAD RAISED

And the dead weren't left out. Wigglesworth himself only claimed that three people came back to life after prayer, but one writer claims this happened on at least fourteen occasions. Once, Wigglesworth was called to the home of a family mourning the loss of a little boy, just five years of age. In those days, the custom was to keep the body at the family home, where friends could pay their last respects, rather than rushing the corpse to funeral directors as now.

Tears ran down Wigglesworth's cheeks as he looked at the boy lying in his coffin. Asking the father to leave the room, he lifted the still form of the lad from the coffin, rebuked death in the name of the Lord Jesus and commanded it to surrender its victim. The child returned to life.

On a second occasion, the pastor of a church asked for Wigglesworth's help. A man in his area had died, but after prayer was raised from the dead. However, the disease that had killed him was still active and the family were told to repent and put matters right within their home. They did, and the Lord healed the man who lived for another thirty years.[25, 26]

KATHRYN KUHLMAN

Kuhlman was the redhead from Missouri who became the foremost female evangelist of the twentieth century. In many ways, her life was difficult. Headstrong, she married the wrong man and later divorced. She came back on track spiritually, but even then she was betrayed by her own staff. Her death, in 1976, was also surrounded by shadowy controversy. Nevertheless, wherever she went, those who thought miracles impossible learned to change their minds.

Believing that her wonderful Lord could meet every need, she began preaching at the Denver Revival Tabernacle under a sign stating "Prayer changes things." Healing services would be held at the end of the evangelistic meetings. In 1947, at Franklin Gospel Tabernacle, a woman came up to her and revealed that the previous night when she had preached, a tumour, diagnosed by her doctor, had been healed. She had returned to the doctor that morning and the healing was verified – the tumour was no longer present. The following Sunday, a World War 1 veteran who had been blinded in one eye twenty-two years previously by a splash of molten metal, prayed, "God, please heal my eye," whilst she was preaching. Two days later, he returned to the tabernacle to testify that he could suddenly see the sun burst forth in all of its glory.

In 1948, she moved to Pittsburgh and the miracles really began to flow. A man whose hip had been crushed in a bulldozer accident had already undergone five unsuccessful operations and a bone graft. Awaiting further surgery, he felt an electric shock while she was preaching, and walked away without his crutches, instantly healed. A boy of five, crippled since birth, began to walk, and a woman in a wheelchair for twelve years did likewise, her husband's face streaming with tears.

The Pittsburgh paper reported many of these miracles, but also stated that, *"For everyone who has proclaimed a cure, a score must have faded off into the darkness, as miserable and heartsick as when they came. But most will be back."* Certainly, not everyone was healed first go. One man, bent and stooped since an accident fourteen years previously, had to attend several services over five months plus give up alcohol and cigarettes before his leg began to vibrate violently during a service. Miss Kuhlman recognised that God was healing him; after the service, he found that his shortened leg had grown out and that his back had loosened. His gratitude led him to work for her for the next 28 years.

PROOF OF HEALINGS

One of the difficulties faced in this field regards the lack of medical proof that physical and other healings have definitely taken place. Indeed, controversy and disbelief over Kuhlman's ministry led to a magazine, Redbook, to assign a Pittsburgh reporter to look into her work. I quote the editor's foreword in full: *No amount of doubt regarding 'faith healing' of any sort, however, could obscure the fact that startling things were happening at Miss Kuhlman's evangelistic services in Pittsburgh. For four months, writers and researchers investigated the healings and cures. If Redbook's investigators erred, it was on the side of scepticism. But as they questioned and studied, the editors' original incredulity gave way to a conviction that the facts demanded publication....*

Physicians' statements, of course, have been difficult to obtain; although a doctor may not personally object to describing a patient's progress under such circumstances, he usually refuses out of deference to the medical profession's wariness of faith healing.

This magazine has in its custody the following confidential documents: twenty testimonials from persons claiming to have been healed: four statements from clergymen supporting Miss Kuhlman's ministry; two letters from public officials; four workmen's compensation reports; two statements from men in fields allied to medical work and six medical and x-ray reports....

C. M. Clark, Pittsburgh's hearing-aid expert, stated in a letter: "We actually saw God's miracle healing" of a deaf-mute who repeated words "using lip forms, throat tones and nasal sounds which she had never experienced."

This magazine therefore invites readers' attention to this report, the integrity of which has been checked in every possible way, confident that persons who have faith, or the hope of it, will find here a message of deep inner significance.

In her last decade, Kuhlman's ministry expanded into Canada. It began, as usual, with a miraculous healing. A 62-year old farmer from Ontario was dying from Hodgkins lymphoma. Cobalt and x-ray treatment failed, as the cancerous lumps returned and spread. Prior to further radical treatment, one of his farming neighbours suggested he attend a miracle service. Told by a man that, *"God can heal you,*

you know," he was hopeful, despite being in great pain. As he tried to enter Carnegie Hall, a total stranger came up to him and said, *"You have cancer, don't you?"* Amazed by her insight, he accepted prayer and indeed prayed himself, *"I am yours, Lord, do with me what you will."* Instantly he felt a strange sensation running through his body and the pain was gone. Later, on the platform, Miss Kuhlman prayed for him; for the next three days, water poured from his skin pores. Returning to Canada, he was pronounced healed by the cancer clinic at the General Hospital in Ottawa. Even his doctor called it a miracle.[27]

REINHARD BONNKE

Bonnke's fifty years of work around the world was celebrated by the publication of his life story in 2009. Starting off as a preacher in Lesotho, Southern Africa, God gave him a new mandate to evangelise the whole of Africa. Preaching to vast numbers of people, his words have frequently been accompanied by dramatic healings. Excerpts from the beginning of his autobiography *Living a Life of Fire* give a flavour of what he sees on a very regular basis: *"It is a tropical night in Northern Nigeria. We are in the heart of Africa. The air is warm and moist and full of sound. A local gospel group performs a melody of praise accompanied by a snakeskin drum. A chorus of birds, frogs and insects joins them from the surrounding trees. The vast crowd standing in front of me radiates heat and expectancy. Nearly 700,000 tribesmen have walked for many miles to this site. Many of them are Muslims. Their upturned faces draw me like a moth to a flame. 2,400,000 will attend in five nights of preaching. More than 1.4 million will accept Jesus as Saviour at the invitations. Follow up teams will disciple each one....*

I see that some in the crowd tonight are crippled. Some lie sick on pallets. Others lean on crutches. Not all will be healed, but some of these crippled will walk. I must tell you, when they walk, I will dance with them across this platform! Wouldn't you? Some are blind, and some of those blind will see. I cannot explain why, but in Muslim areas I see more blind eyes open. I wish everyone could be with me to see it. Chronic pain leaves bodies, cancerous growths disappear. These are but a few of the signs that follow the preaching of the good news.

He started in Maseru, the capital city of Lesotho. God told him through the Holy Spirit to call the totally blind; in faith, he did so, telling them that he would pray, that their eyes would be opened and they would see a white man standing before them. As he shouted out, *"In the name of Jesus, blind eyes open!"* a woman, whom he would later learn had been blind for four years, cried, *"I see, I see, I see."* A young boy with twisted limbs was then passed forward from the back of the room, hand to hand. As Bonnke held the youngster, he saw the twisted limbs and forgot to pray. Nevertheless, his body began to vibrate and he slipped out of the German's hands, landing on his feet, and began to run around. Learning that day that the Holy Spirit heals, all things became possible.

Later, in Namibia, another man asked him to pray for his ears. He had cancer in one ear and no eardrum in the other, but after prayer, jumped up and down as hearing returned to the ear with no drum. Bonnke could only conclude that the Creator must have spare parts, because in this case there was nothing there to heal.

As his reputation for miracles began to grow throughout Southern Africa, Bonnke was not happy. Positioned by God to help save Africa, he described himself as a salvation evangelist who also prays for the sick, not a healing evangelist. Salvation is ultimately more important than healing, although healing often follows preaching of the gospel. And as people were healed, news travelled like wildfire. In South Africa, miracles of healing led many who came on crutches to leave them behind; there were so many that they were heaped up into a large pile. And the healings weren't restricted to black Africans. Bonnke heard about one wealthy white lady from Pretoria who was dying from cancer. She had been listening to one of his cassette tapes about healing. After prayer, she sensed she had been healed and a complete battery of tests a week later at the Cancer Research Institute proved negative. The doctors were unable to explain it. A year later she contacted him to say that she was cured from cancer. Sadly, she died from another unsuspected cause soon after.

Bonnke, like Wigglesworth, was not against doctors. Believing that God granted medical knowledge to the world to help us, and that some amazing cures are brought about by medics and medicines, he would simply say that God is for our health, not against it. Equally, he has never claimed to fully understand what God is up to. Surrounded by dramatic miracles, prayers for his own mother did not lead to improvement and tested his faith. But he had always prayed on the principle of obeying the Word of God, not because he fully understood it. Not having all the answers, some questions were too big for him so he left them in God's hands.

He would, however, be taught one more important lesson by God. In 1983, he was in Perth, Australia. Asking the Lord what He would do in the auditorium, his eyes were drawn to a woman in a wheelchair. Told by God that she would be healed that night, he decided to announce her healing in advance over the microphone, with Channel 4 news team eagerly recording it. But the woman did not take what she heard as good news, hiding her head in her hands. The atmosphere amongst the crowd grew cool; what Bonnke did not realise was that the woman was an invited guest but wasn't religious, with no expectation of healing. Until then, his understanding had always been that if Jesus credited miracles of healing to the faith of the sick person, so should he.

At that moment, asking the Lord how this would work, the Holy Spirit told him, *"Today it's not her faith, it's your faith. You are going to see a great miracle."* Immediately, the faith of the friends of the paralysed man who was lowered through a hole in a roof to meet Jesus, came to mind. The Bible does not record any faith of his own, merely that of his friends. Basing his sermon on that text, at the end he commanded her to get up and walk. With brittle bone disease, standing up should have caused her bones to crack. Indeed, her doctors had told her she would never walk again. But rising to her feet, she followed his instruction and began to run, taking off like a shot and screaming with laughter. Years later, she attended a banquet to show him that she remained totally healed. No more broken bones, a child of God set free – another example of God's love and amazing grace.

Bonnke comments, *"Today, when I pray for someone and that person is not healed, I do not blame it on a lack of faith. The longer I live, the less I pretend to know about the mind of God. I do not know why some are healed and others are not. I only know that sometimes it is the faith of a sick person that makes them whole, and sometimes it is the faith of others."* [28]

NICKY CRUZ

Cruz initially came to public attention as a gang leader from Brooklyn, who had personally killed sixteen rival gang members. This phase of his life is described in the classic book *Run Baby Run*. His dramatic conversion changed everything. As a Christian evangelist, he returned to work particularly with those whose lifestyles he understood only too well.

Leading masses to Christ over the past thirty years, he has witnessed extraordinary physical and emotional healings.

But such healings were never his primary intention. First and foremost he was an evangelist. In 1962, a woman rang him as he was preparing to speak in a church in Brooklyn. Her seven year-old daughter had been crippled since birth and she wanted Cruz to pray for her that evening. Advising her of his job description, he told the mother not to get her hopes up. Healing was not then part of his ministry; but the woman was persistent and rang him a second time, convinced that he could heal her daughter and that they must look out for each other. Wary of her forcefulness and of potential embarrassment, he intended to do no such thing and even prayed that they wouldn't make it to the meeting! But they did, and stood before him for prayer. Scared, and not wanting to let anyone down, he asked another pastor to pray, but was told that her request involved him! Holding the frail little girl in his arms, he opened his mouth but the only word emerging was *"Jesus."* At that moment, he felt her joints and muscles move and strengthen, the bones cracking and her legs swelling. Suddenly, she was walking, eyes wide open and beaming. Not sure what to do, he left the building before the service ended, shocked by the mother's amazing faith and the miracle! Following that night, he would see many people healed as God worked through him or those around him.

He was once asked, *"Do you really think we can make a difference for Christ in the inner cities?"* He answered, *"Yes ... and not just the inner cities but in every neighbourhood in every corner of the world."* Drawing on his street background, Cruz set up an organization called Teen Challenge, dedicated to helping youngsters get off drugs and replace them with Jesus. The work could be exhausting; two days and nights he looked after Sonny, from Harlem, who was in desperate pain as he came off drugs. Finally falling asleep, Cruz woke the next morning to hear Sonny crying: *"God did it, Nicky. He cleaned me up and saved me. I asked him this morning to come into my heart, and he did. My heart is clean and white, just like the snow outside. I feel so pure, Nicky. God has forgiven me; I know He has. I'm free. I don't ever want to go back to my life of sin and drugs."* Cold turkey stopped in its tracks.

Another man screamed in pain just outside his office; he, too, was drying out from drugs. Placing his hand on his forehead, Cruz prayed that Jesus would give him relief and peace and sleep. Immediately, the man's face became calm, the shaking stopped and within minutes he was asleep. Another miracle, and one seen by a writer researching his ministry. Nevertheless, this man couldn't believe that what he had just witnessed was God's doing. Cruz comments that he often forgot how strange and unbelievable the works of the Spirit can be to others.

Many years later, God called him back to the inner cities, saying, *"I want you to go back where you started, to the people who need you most. Take my message of forgiveness to the streets, and I will show my power and strength to them in ways they can never forget or deny."*

In 1985, he held a crusade in Mexico City, just after an earthquake had left much of the city in ruins. On the first night, a deaf and dumb girl began to speak after prayer; her first word was: *"Jesus."* Another woman made her way to the front. Deformed and misshapen, she couldn't even lift her head, but after one of the workers prayed, she straightened and stood upright. Whether Cruz was an evangelist or a healer mattered not – God, this night, decided to heal bodies. The next man who came forward had a tumour the size of a football protruding from his stomach. As several workers prayed, the growth shrank before their eyes and then disappeared. Calling for anyone who was sick to stand, he asked believers around them to lay hands on them and pray. Throughout the auditorium, people shouted and screamed for joy. They lost count of the number healed that evening, but all were eyewitnesses to God's power.

Healing comes in different forms. Crippled children and addicts healed on the spot are spectacular, but emotional healing may also be critical. Abusive and alcoholic fathers left his crusades free of their anger and frustration, never to pick up a bottle or lift their hand against their loved ones again. Couples on the verge of divorce, hating and resenting each other, would leave with a deep sense of forgiveness and a renewed vision for their marriage. Each came looking for help and found healing through the work of the Holy Spirit. Their lives, too, would never be the same again.[29]

ROLLAND AND HEIDI BAKER

Rolland had always wanted to believe that miracles could be a normal part of the Christian life, with God always providing enough of what was needed. Missing out on this, he felt, would represent the worst possible fate. Seeking God deeply, he needed a partner in ministry to share such a daring faith. And God provided Heidi. She was also fiercely determined to serve God. They spent their honeymoon in Indonesia, having bought a one-way ticket and with just a few dollars in their pockets. Today, they oversee over 5,000 churches in one of the poorest countries in the world. People in Mozambique have suffered terribly from war and natural disasters, but are desperate for Jesus. Entering the country in January 1995, just after the war was over, they began by taking in unwanted children. With almost nothing of their own to provide, they would see God supply all the children's needs, not least by multiplying food as it was given out in the manner of the disciples feeding the 5,000. And God's provision, just as Rolland had dreamt, would also extend to miraculous healings.

The first major miracle that Heidi saw in her church was spectacular. During a three-day fast, a man came and told her that his wife had died from AIDS. Inside the house, everyone was crying. Praying for a miracle, she felt great power enter her. Telling everyone to stop crying, they sang and worshipped the Lord and then she prayed for the dead mother. After an hour, the very cold body began to warm up and then the woman vomited. By the third hour of prayer, her whole body began to move and they took her into the church; as they spent the entire night in prayer, she began to speak. Her husband was converted right away!

One of her fellow pastors had a similar experience with a woman who had died from cholera. Heidi's eyes were opened to what was possible, and they weren't the only ones. She would comment, *"For the first time in my life I saw totally blind eyes, white from cataracts, change colour and become normal and healthy. We do our best to preach the Word clearly, and as signs and wonders follow, the remotest and most forgotten of the African bush are being added to the church."*

Perhaps the reason that signs and wonders became so manifest was that the people wanted Jesus so badly. Alongside the devastating flood in March 2000, which lead to the biggest humanitarian aid mobilisation ever in Africa, the people of Mozambique were tired of the devastating effects of witchcraft, paganism and ancestor worship. Instead, they wanted to hear from the living God. Heidi noted that, *"They wanted the Truth, nothing less. They begged for church, for preaching, for Bibles and for prayer."* Indeed, they thronged past food sacks to get their hands on tracts. *"Spiritual fervour among the flood victims shot up. They found out Jesus could drive out demons, heal the sick, and replace witch doctors*

*with grace, beauty and love. They wanted Bibles more than
rice and blankets, more than anything. We'd arrive, and
they'd cry, 'Let's have church!'"*

Following the rains, in 2001 there was a bad outbreak of
cholera. Within days, seventy of Heidi's children, pastors
and workers were taken to a big tent – the "cholera hospital."
She thinks the disease started when contaminated food was
brought into her church for a wedding. Terrified of a city-
wide epidemic, the Minister of Health told her, *"You will
be responsible for killing half of Maputo."* It looked like
their centre and ministry would be shut down. Washing and
disinfecting everything, her staff were exhausted. Every day,
she spent hours with the infected children, holding them,
soaking them in prayer and declaring that they would live.
As they vomited on her and looked like death, doctors were
concerned that she would die along with them. Rolland later
said they were ready to quit if God didn't do something.

Their entire future in Mozambique was under threat,
but intensive prayer from around the world started to reap
reward. Children began to return from the hospital, there
were no new cases and then all were home. Cholera had gone,
Heidi was fine and the doctors and nurses were in shock.
The Director of Health, confronted by the evidence, changed
his tune: *"This is God. The only reason you got through this
was God! You and dozens of these children should be dead."*
Eight of his medical staff immediately wanted to change jobs
and work with them after seeing that not one of her flock in
the hospital had been lost.

In tough times persistence was crucial. Heidi had received
many prophecies over the years that the blind would see, the
deaf would hear, the crippled would walk, and so on. Blind
people were everywhere in such a poor nation, and Heidi
would go up to them, offering prayer. They all accepted
Jesus as Saviour, but at least the first twenty people failed

to see. But she didn't give up. With another missionary, she attended a little mud church up north. As they prayed for a blind lady, she fell to the ground and her eyes changed colour from white to grey to brown and she began to see.

The next blind man they came across didn't see, but others would be healed; later, in another remote town, Heidi had a word of knowledge from the Lord that deaf ears were about to be opened. In a small crowd of 500, ears were indeed opened and word got out – 10,000 turned up at the next meeting. No-one asked for prayer for minor aches; instead, the deaf, blind and dumb came expecting miracles.[30]

BILL JOHNSON

Johnson is an American who challenges all Christians to believe that the supernatural should be part of a normal Christian life. This is what happens when heaven invades earth, believers seeing extraordinary miracles in their everyday lives. The Kingdom of God then moves from being a future hope to a present reality. One pastor wrote that he wished he had come across such a practical demonstration of faith 50 years earlier, when he began work. Johnson himself aims to spend the rest of his life seeing *"... impossibilities bow to the name of Jesus. All my eggs are in one basket. There is no Plan B."* As a result, his life and that of his church act as a death-blow to those who think that the age of miracles is over.

Jesus' first recorded miracle came at a wedding, turning water into wine. Johnson was at a wedding when he was told that someone there had less than three years to live. By this point in his ministry, miracles of healing had become common, to the point that life-threatening diseases were seen more as potential miracles than something to fear. The man in question wore braces on each arm, had a large neck brace and walked with difficulty. Carpal tunnel syndrome caused numbness and pain in his hands, whilst a bad accident had led to an artificial shin and hip in a shortened leg. Finally, cancer had caused him to lose muscles in his neck. After prayer, the man began to move his hands freely and his leg grew visibly, enabling him to walk without a limp. Finally, another member of the church, a doctor, commanded new muscles to grow in his neck, giving each their correct Latin names. As his neck began to move, the patient exclaimed, *"The lumps are gone."* The doctor was able to give him a clean bill of health and the man and his wife became Christians. Within weeks he got a job, his first in seventeen years. His healing was complete.

A woman with oesophageal cancer was healed during a Sunday service. No prayer on this occasion, but as she felt the fire of God touch her, she concluded that healing was taking place. Her doctor was initially sceptical: *"This kind does not go away"* – but, after examining her, concluded, *"Not only do you not have cancer, you have a new oesophagus."* Her miracle was the result of corporate faith tugging on heaven. Johnson teaches members of his church to live out their faith and the youth are not excepted. One student was ordering fast food when he saw three men in a car arrive at the drive-in window. Chatting with them, he noticed the man in the back seat had a broken leg. So he climbed in, invited the Holy Spirit to come and wasn't put off when the man cursed, not understanding the holy fire on his leg! But as they all got out, the man removed the brace and stomped his leg, completely healed. The men were so affected that they opened the car boot, tipped out narcotics and destroyed them, before being led to Christ. The normal Christian life. But it wasn't always like this for Johnson.

In 1987, he attended a conference on signs and wonders, led by John Wimber in California. He left discouraged, for whilst they shared the same doctrine, only Wimber's people were seeing fruit. He learnt that correct teaching must be followed with action, faith spelt RISK. Things changed immediately; his church prayed and saw miracles, but many were not healed and, again discouragement set in and the risk-taking decreased. Attending the Toronto Blessing in 1995, he vowed that if God touched him again, he would never back off. He did and Johnson fulfilled his promise. The manifestation of the gifts of the Holy Spirit have become the sole purpose for his existence.

One Sunday evening, after prayer, praise and teaching, it was time to ask God for miracles. A man started jumping up and down, and exclaiming. His trousers seemed too big for him and he had to hold them up. The team learnt that he had been given by doctors two weeks to live because of tumours. He was healed that night. Johnson comments, *"In his mind, we were the last stop on the way to heaven or on the way to a miracle."* Now all he needed was a new wardrobe!

A woman drove to Bill Johnson's church from two States away, struggling to breathe from likely lung cancer. Having had to be helped into the building, she left pain free and able to breathe without restriction. Another victory over the enemy.

Not all Christians believe this is possible. Bad teaching over many years can rob believers of the joy of experiencing God's power. Turning this on its head, Johnson actively teaches about signs and wonders and has set up a school of ministry in which people learn to operate in the supernatural, outside the church walls. One day after class, students went hospital visiting. A lady with a brain tumour was deaf in one ear and was losing feeling on one side of her body. Slurring her words, she spoke with great difficulty and was in terrible pain. This time the students sang, expressing their love to the Lord. The deafness left, her speech became clearer and she began moving her limbs, exclaiming, *"All the pain is gone."*

Johnson comments that, *"God overhauled her body when a worship service broke out around her..."* and that, *"This is normal Christianity. Miracles are normal."*

Another lady who had had five operations in just under five years following an accident, was told by doctors that her shortened arm with no feeling would probably simply dangle for the rest of her life. But prayer restored the arm to normal. Reaching to pick up her two-year old girl, she was told, *"No Mummy, broken arm."*

"It's OK, honey," she replied, and the little girl smiled hugely as her mum, for the first time, lifted her up.

At a service in California, healing again broke out. Out of the two hundred in the congregation, forty to fifty acknowledged that God healed their bodies that night. A woman with a destroyed optic nerve began to see. A deaf person was healed, as was a woman bound to a wheelchair through crippling arthritis. A child with a club foot was healed. Another time, a woman came for prayer, having been told that her baby had died in the womb and was due to be removed the next week. The person praying discerned from God that the child was alive, and doctors, who had diagnosed death, were dumbfounded as the child was now alive.

I would like to finish this chapter with one of my favourite stories. One of Johnson's missionaries was travelling in Africa, when the small bus ahead of her careered off the road and crashed at about 60 m.p.h. Passengers were thrown from the vehicle as it rolled; for onlookers, the site was gruesome. Many had life-threatening injuries, were unconscious, and one woman was clearly dead. With no vital signs, her head was also facing her back and one eye lay on her cheek. The missionary had previously graduated as a physician's assistant. Placing each bystander in charge of one of the victims, she instructed them to, *"Speak life in Jesus' name. When I look over at you, I want to see your lips moving."*

And move they did. Minutes later, the woman assigned to the dead passenger screamed as the woman groaned, turned her head around and began to breathe. Her misplaced eye was also back in its socket! This caused the others to pray all the more earnestly, and within a short time all those unconscious had regained consciousness and serious wounds stopped bleeding. Many were healed and those who should have died were spared.

Johnson states that when he heard this story, he remembered others who had prayed even when the situation seemed hopeless. Commenting that this is the attitude we need in troubling circumstances, whether they last for days, months or even years, he recommends that we always declare the faithfulness and goodness of God. God is good all the time, and He, *"...forgives all your sins and heals all your diseases"* (Psalm 103:3). [31]

Chapter Nine

WHO WILL PRAY FOR ME?

Therefore confess your sins to each other and pray for each other so that you may be healed. The prayer of a righteous man is powerful and effective.[32]

The previous chapter, in one sense, was easy to write. All of the healers chosen were familiar to me through their books, and some I had seen in action personally. An element of bias towards them I cannot deny, but familiarity did make the job of choosing whom to pick somewhat easier for there are plenty of other evangelists, pray-ers and pastors worldwide who also report healings on a regular basis. Truly, the prayers of righteous men and women are powerful and effective. Unashamedly, I've given you examples from my favourites although it wasn't easy deciding what to include with space allowing me just a few extraordinary events per person; nevertheless, I have tried to paint as broad a picture as possible of what God has been up to.

So no apologies for my selection, which shows clearly that even today the blind see, the deaf hear, the lame walk and those who have died are being raised. Remarkable? Yes. Surprising? It shouldn't be. Jesus said, towards the end of his time on earth, *"Believe me when I say that I am in the Father and the Father is in me; or at least believe on the evidence of the miracles themselves. I tell you the truth, anyone who has faith in me will do what I have been doing. He will do even greater things than these, because I am going to the Father."* [33]

"...anyone who has faith in me...." These evangelists and healers have taken Jesus the Son of God absolutely at his word. Knowing that God's healing power is available to believers through the Holy Spirit, they have deliberately, intentionally and desperately sought to heal the sick through prayer in Jesus' name. Each one candidly admits that not everyone who is prayed for is healed. But like the South African golfer, Gary Player, who was accused of being lucky and responded that it was a funny thing, "The harder I practise, the luckier I get", they have prayed and prayed when nothing seemed to happen, until they discovered the truth written in Matthew 7:7, *"Ask and it will be given to you; seek and you will find...."* Not put off by any initial "failures", they continued to seek, continued to take God's Word seriously, and seen healing flow.

One crucial common element is that all healing is requested in Jesus' Name. When allied to his promise above, it is no shock that healings mimic those of the Saviour; but what did Jesus mean when he spoke of believers doing *"even greater things"*? After all, it's hard to top his personal miracles, when you consider that these included raising a man, Lazarus, a full four days after his death. The quality of his miracles is therefore not in question. Instead, he was surely referring to a greater quantity of miracles, through the number of workers he foresaw involved. In this context, with all diseases and even death itself subject to his authority, is it any wonder that cancer, the dreaded disease, the big one, is also under God's control?

Now I am into good news, but I am also realistic. I am delighted that many tens of thousands have been cured when attending evangelistic-healing meetings, and that God has allowed this gift of healing to extend beyond a meeting place to those far off, sometimes using prayed-over handkerchiefs or other articles. But some of those detailed – Wigglesworth and Kuhlman – have died. Others like Bonnke, Cruz and the Bakers do most of their work far away from the average Briton or American. And Bill Johnson cannot be everywhere! How can the average man or woman who develops cancer in the West access supernatural healing today?

British governments, from whichever party, often claim that they wish to decentralise power. Less top-down decision-making, more power to the people. It doesn't always work, but the concept is sound and it applies even more pertinently to supernatural healing. God the Holy Trinity allows believers to exercise the power to heal, and the power is from Him. Some mistakenly believe that Jesus' promise of miracles was aimed purely at his twelve disciples and for that time period only, but such a restriction fails to account for the evidence before us today. Equally importantly, Jesus never intended his dozen closest men to be succeeded by only a few favoured healing-evangelists today. On the contrary, following Pentecost, God's power to heal has been available to *all* believers. So whilst I get very excited about the ministries of those who are clearly being used by God in this area, logically they should not be the only vehicles through whom God chooses to heal today.

A man called Nicodemus sought out Jesus one night. Referring to his miraculous deeds, Nicodemus asked many questions and received teaching concerning the Holy Spirit which applies to all of us today. Jesus explained that, *"The wind blows wherever it pleases. You hear its sound, but you cannot tell where it comes from or where it is going. So it is with everyone born of the Spirit."*

Clearly, the Spirit is not under our control. Living and

active, He turns up wherever and whenever He decides, surprising and delighting us always and involving new people along the way. In the past few years, He appears to have been at work in many different settings where people testify to have been healed in Jesus' name. Of course, all such claims must be verified and the teaching checked against Scripture, but it does appear that miraculous healing is demonstrably present throughout the world today, as God always intended. We look at a few examples of such settings here.

In America, in April 2008, what became known as the "Florida Outpouring" led to many being healed from around the world. As with an earlier (and very different) anointing alighting on Toronto in 1994, some of those attending took the anointing home with them. Offshoots grew around the world, greatly increasing the scope for healing beyond the original focus. No need for handkerchiefs any more; God uses our television and internet age to heal remotely through broadcasting, as we saw earlier in relation to Benny Hinn's ministry. Something significant was happening, and like thousands of others, I wanted a piece of it. A family holiday in Florida provided the excuse. On my return home, I determined to see whether the outpouring was genuinely transferrable by visiting a church in the West Midlands that had been highly blessed by their time in Florida. For many months this church needed to run healing sessions every night of the week (bar one when they recovered) to cope with the hundreds each day either seeking healing or supporting those who did. That particular night, expectation and faith ran high and several people reported some improvement in their chronic conditions as a result.

Millions attending the evangelists worldwide, thousands showing up nightly in Florida, and now hundreds in Dudley, West Midlands, and other offshoots around the world – the numbers maybe reducing but the opportunity for healing is increasing as healing becomes more local. Bill Johnson's School of Supernatural Ministry adopts a similar approach, attracting students worldwide who then apply in their home situations what they have learnt. Last year, I was introduced to another English doctor, Peter Carter, who had spent three months with his wife learning from Johnson's team in Redding, California. As a result, he set up the School of Supernatural Ministry in North Kent, a natural offshoot of what the Spirit had begun in America. Decentralisation allows God's healing work to reach far more people than simply by relying on the ministries of those few with special anointing.

But again, a dose of realism. Whilst it's OK for me to beetle about, checking out healing centres and getting charged up spiritually, what about those who are stuck where they are? In my area of east Kent, many are too old, too poor, lack mobile friends, or are otherwise disinclined to travel beyond their local area; others may be confined to their house or bedroom through illness. For all of them, Florida might as well be on the moon, and even north-west Kent is an unbridgeable forty-odd miles away. Lacking awareness that help may be just a few clicks away on their television, how can these people receive healing prayer? The answer is further decentralisation – prayer "on the doorstep". Let me give a few examples known to me personally.

Some years ago, I was part of a mission team in Maasai-land, Kenya. One evening at supper, the Maasai pastor overseeing our work asked whether any of our team had prayed for a child with club feet. Wondering what was up, two members raised their hands. As an evangelistic team, our explicit mission was to preach, not heal, but the mother of this particular child had a different agenda. With no hospital treatment possible, this poor lady saw our team as the only hope for her child. Talking to her led to prayer for the baby. With no instant healing apparent, the team members carried on their business, but later that same day, the baby's newly straightened feet became the talk of the village.

This African child received healing because Christians brought it with them. The mother did her bit by allowing us to pray; her faith, and that of the team, was suitably rewarded. But in instances where the sick cannot exit their own home, healing prayer must be brought to them. Maggie Hughes is a member of our church prayer team, but by profession a district nurse. Some years ago, she visited an elderly lady who was blind in both eyes from macular degeneration. Nellie would sit in her wicker chair in her porch, and as Maggie arrived, she would call out to the old lady in order not to startle her.

One day, Maggie had a deep conviction in her heart that she should pray for her patient. Indeed, the desire was so strong that she was unable to move from where she was standing until she had done so. She describes it as if the Holy Spirit had made her shoes leaden like concrete, fixing her to the spot. Asking Nellie what she would like prayer for, she was told, *"I would like God to restore my sight so that I may get my affairs in order."* Prayer followed, in which Maggie asked the Holy Spirit to come in power, restore her sight and bless her with His comfort and peace. Nellie recounted that she felt warm and peaceful afterwards, but there was no obvious immediate healing. Nevertheless, Maggie told her that God would never abandon her, that she should carry on asking Him for healing, and offered to pray again during the next visit.

Some time later, this visit took place. Sensing on this occasion that she should not call out, Maggie was overjoyed to see Nellie waving frantically at her. Not only could she see, but she had a book in her lap! When she returned to the practice where she worked, she discovered a hospital letter from Nellie's ophthalmologist which stated,

"This lady was blind but now she sees. There is no medical explanation for this but she tells me she has received prayer. I can only suggest that she continues in this way."

Maggie writes, *"Jesus wants his children and his disciples to be whole and to be known for it. There is no greater joy in all the world than to see God at work healing and restoring His creation."*

Some, like Nellie and the Maasai lady are keen for prayer. In parts of the African bush, what else is there? Others are more reluctant, and some may only turn to God for healing as a last resort; either way, their lives may never be the same again.

Margaret Lubbock is my godmother. An old university friend of my parents, she had suffered from an increasingly bad back in the 1970s. As it stiffened, with sciatica thrown in for good measure, she was reduced to crawling on her hands and knees to the toilet, before bed rest became inevitable. Depression set in, as many months of conventional and alternative healing proved fruitless. A leading back specialist suggested that surgery to remove several discs and fuse the spine might help, but could well leave her worse off.

Just before this, Margaret and her husband Bill had come to the Lord. Her pastor came to see her, and although admitting that he had never done this sort of thing before, suggested that he pray for her healing. As he began to pray in tongues, she felt immense power like electricity go through her. She felt a "motor" start up in her right hip and then her shortened right leg grew, seemingly too far as it outgrew the left leg; at this point, the motor transferred to her left hip, allowing that leg to catch up perfectly. Shouting, *"Praise God, He's healed me,"* she shot out of bed and landed on her feet. Utterly joyful, bearing in mind that she'd been unable to move to the right or left in bed for fifteen months, she felt as if a straitjacket had been removed; literally leaping about, she now felt something happen to her lower discs and was sure that God was rebuilding them too.

Three weeks later, she returned to see her bone specialist, who confirmed that her back, her discs, her ligaments, the muscle tone and even her ankle reflex, previously lost through damage to the sciatic nerve, had returned to normal. Astounded, he remarked, *"No doctor in the world could do that,"* and she replied, *"Praise the Lord."*

"Indeed, I think that's who you should praise. I have had no hand in this." He went on to say that he had seen miracle cures done by the Lord a few times before and wished for more, so he could retire from practice altogether! Another doctor present, there to study his methods, said absolutely nothing, his jaw dropping open in amazement.

Since that day, Margaret, Bill, the pastor and indeed the church itself, have all had a significant healing ministry.[35]

Blindness and a bad back – well worth relieving, but this is a book about cancer. Do I have any personal experience of cancer being healed? As Christian GPs, my wife and I will often pray for patients with either incurable conditions or awful social situations. Heather has recently seen four long-term infertile couples conceive, with the only difference in their treatment being added prayer. Equally, one of her patients with lung cancer only recently died, many years beyond her expected date, following prayer. Naturally, we cannot prove that prayer made a difference here – for there was no exact "control" patient to compare her with. And, in truth, I can think of several patients, Christians all, who have died from cancer despite much prayer. Two were teenage boys, whose faith was remarkable; I don't pretend to be able to explain why God chose not to prolong their young lives on this earth.

But the example of a teenage girl does provide hope and a reason to pray. Up to now, I've concentrated on people receiving prayer from others, whether at conferences, in meetings, remotely or in their home situations. But this girl prayed for herself. Many years ago, I was a junior surgeon in Cambridge when the 15-year old girl was admitted whilst I was on call. She had an abdominal mass, sufficiently serious for the consultant to operate on her that evening. What took place is known in the trade as an "open and shut job". Her belly was a mass of tumour, the origin unclear but with extensive spread obvious. All that was possible was a biopsy and closure. No debulking of the mass would have made any difference to her outlook.

The next morning, surrounded by his entourage including myself, the consultant came round to give her the bad news. Never a pleasant part of the job, her tender age made what lay ahead all the more poignant. But instead of the usual post-op picture, he found her sitting up in bed and wearing a huge grin. As he started to explain where she was at and the implications for the future, she stopped him; *"No need to go any further, the lump has gone. I've been praying...."*

A quick glance at her abdomen revealed the surgical scar but no underlying lump. Unable to explain the situation and for once at a loss and thoroughly out of control of the situation, the boss gave orders for her to be rapidly discharged. No follow up, no biopsy result, the girl was quickly forgotten as we thoughtlessly moved on to the next case. But that lump, assumed to be malignant from prior experience, had simply disappeared.

In the UK, perhaps because of a national cultural characteristic of reticence, we are often reluctant to pray for ourselves. So many people I have come across are more than happy to pray for others, but not for themselves. It is somehow seen as wrong, or selfish, even disrespectful of others with greater needs. Perhaps one's outlook changes when cancer supervenes, for, in all honesty, our own difficulties are clearly worthy of prayer. That girl who was healed certainly did pray for herself, and look at what God did when she prayed! Again, we shouldn't be surprised. One of my favourite paragraphs in the Old Testament concerns a poor man named Jabez. His name meant "pain", a sad reflection on his life. *Jabez was more honourable than his brothers. His mother had named him Jabez, saying, "I gave birth to him in pain." Jabez cried out to the God of Israel, "Oh, that you would bless me and enlarge my territory! Let your hand be with me, and keep me from harm so that I will be free from pain." And God granted his request.*[36]

When times are hard, people more readily see the need to pray. Some think it wrong to call out to God when they are in trouble, having not done so previously. Certainly, God wants a relationship with us at all times, but often it takes a calamity like cancer to bring Him to our attention. C.S. Lewis once described pain as God's megaphone – His way of getting through to us. And as the statistics and stories have shown, having God on our side in times of trouble is well worth it. And this applies whether we are an ordinary citizen or the leader of our country.

During the Second World War, in one of the darkest moments in English history, more than 300,000 British troops were pinned down in northern France. With inadequate ammunition and supplies, and with Nazi forces bearing down on them, all that was needed was for Hitler to say the word and a ferocious attack would lead to their certain annihilation. Prime Minister Winston Churchill summed up the situation. He knew that, at best, the navy could rescue a maximum of

20,000 to 30,000 men before it was too late. And even worse, if that were possible, with so many forces wiped out, Hitler would then invade Britain and win.

But all was not lost. King George V1 called for a national day of prayer. That Sunday, an estimated 70% of British people begged for God's mercy for their fathers and their sons and for national survival, at churches all over the country. And the Lord heard those heartfelt prayers. Inexplicably, Hitler delayed giving the order to his generals to finish the enemy off, and also a great storm passed over Germany, preventing Nazi planes from taking off and assisting them. The English Channel, however, was still and calm, allowing 900 fishing boats, yachts, trawlers and other private and government vessels to ferry the troops back from the French beaches. By the grace of God, nearly one third of a million men were saved. The withdrawal at Dunkirk is generally recognised as a miracle, with Churchill himself calling it a "miracle of deliverance". But more was needed and God stepped in again.

A few months later, the German airforce was poised to invade Britain. Germany had almost 2,800 aircraft against 900 British fighters and Hermann Goering promised Hitler that the Luftwaffe could destroy the RAF prior to a full invasion. Beginning in August 1940, the situation looked bleak as the Battle of Britain began, with 25% of our pilots lost in the first 12 days. Goering then changed tactics, switching from attacking airfields to damaging control centres and even though the Luftwaffe were also losing planes, they were coping more easily due to their numerical superiority and Hitler was itching to invade before the good September weather was over.

The war rapidly escalated after a German airman, tired and in a fog over London, accidentally dropped a bomb on a civilian rather than a military target. Churchill was incensed and the following night the RAF raided Berlin, which in turn led Hitler to bomb London. The Blitz began on September 7th, 1940. The pounding would last for 57 nights, but the key event, known as "Battle of Britain Day", would take place on September 15th. Seven days before this day, the King again called the nation to prayer. Despite Christianity being in decline in those days, with God blamed for the carnage of the two World Wars, nevertheless a spark remained and the churches were again packed to the rafters as the country prayed like never before. The result was extraordinary.

Churchill, in his war memoirs, writes of visiting the RAF Operations Room on September 15th. As he watched the battle progressing in the skies, he asked the Air Marshal, "What other reserves have we?" and received the answer, "There are none." But after just five more minutes, he noted that the German bombers and fighters were moving east. No new attacks were taking place. The enemy had had enough and were going home, snatching defeat from the jaws of victory. The Battle of Britain had ended and Hitler never invaded our country.

But someone might rightly point out that the power of God is not like a "tap" we turn on and off. Life in Christ is always shown in the Bible (and this is borne out in Christian experience) to be relational, not "mechanistic". We must not treat God as a "slot machine", for He is personal. That is extremely important when we consider the Christian account of what prayer is all about. The Scriptures, His self-revelation, use *personal* terms to describe His character, not mechanical terms. His acts and promises (some of which are conditional) are personal, not like an impersonal "force".

It is true that part of Jesus' commission to His disciples was a command, to fulfil which an empowering was added at Pentecost. Moreover, the New Testament speaks of "gifts" of healing, amongst other gifts. But the *tasks* disciples are given to do (including healing the sick) are not independent of their *relationship to Him* as their Lord and Master, and not unrelated to the authentic "good news" we read of in the New Testament. When disciples fulfil Jesus' commands and the commission He gives them, they need to go on walking in a close relationship of obedience to Him. That is as true today as it was in the first century. He delegates some authority which is then to be exercised – not independently but in His Name, which means under His lordship or governance. But all too often, this great truth is inverted, God is depicted as being *our* servant rather than our being under the lordship of Jesus, under the direction of the Holy Spirit. How easy it is for such things to be misunderstood!

Some sufferers turn to Him only when the chips are down but ignore Him the rest of the time. Turning to Him in crisis is not wrong, of course, and indeed is to be encouraged, but that has to become a life commitment, not just a quickly forgotten episode. It can be as serious a mistake as thinking that a Christian *beginning* is everything, when the Bible is very clear that *persevering* and *enduring* and *overcoming* are also of crucial importance.

But what do we know of God's attitude to mankind? First, we need to know something of His nature, His character. He has revealed that He is absolutely perfect, just, fair – in the language of the Bible, He is *righteous*. Because we human beings by nature are not like that ourselves, and we have never encountered absolute perfection in this world, we do find that hard to comprehend. Few really understand there is such a gulf between God's perfection and our imperfection! The astonishing thing is that He once did something for us that we could never have done for ourselves. The word used in the Bible to describe that act has a singular form, referring to a once-for-all event, which was a special kind of love which means in this case a single, utterly undeserved and generous act that provided exactly what all needed. God "loved" the world by giving Jesus – Himself God and perfect man – to die in our place, taking what *we all deserved* for our failure to match his perfect standards, ignoring Him, our Creator, failing to acknowledge Him and thank Him for our lives. He gave us an opportunity then to turn to Him in repentance and faith, allowing Him to change us. What Christians mean when they talk about being "saved" is being saved from the penalty of all our sins, and then living "in Christ", which is a completely new dimension of life. So it is both that the Son of God (voluntarily) chose to die in our place, and that He was raised by His Father to life, so that we might have life in Him for ever, rather than death and hell.

That is a brief summary of *how* God loved us. That's not the only issue, though, the real question is *how we respond to what He did for us*. Our love for Him is, quite simply, to be reflected in believing in Jesus whom the Father sent, and obeying His words with the help of His Spirit. When we repent toward God, believe in His Son Jesus and are immersed in His Holy Spirit, we begin to experience a new life in Him, we are born of the Spirit and become a new creation and start to operate under His rule rather than that of Satan. That explains why no Christian should ever think of Christian healing or Christian prayer as *mechanical* or like the operation of a "slot machine".

In the light of these revealed truths, we can see that being healed (precious as that was, and is, for those whose accounts of healing we have recounted, and countless others) is not actually the most important thing, but rather it is the way the healed person (or any of us!) lives the rest of life that matters. And that is not so much about what they "do" but how they then live *in relationship to God in a new life lived in Christ*.

In summary, many sense something of the horrible cruelty seen in crucifixion, but fewer realise that that it was your sins and mine that necessitated such a saving, sacrificial death, and that it was the means God Himself used to provide for our reconciliation. A holy, perfectly just God could not merely "wink" at evil or say "There, there, it doesn't really matter." If He did, He wouldn't be righteous and just.

Whether or not you share this understanding, in actual fact it is His consistent *self-revelation*. The people who have personally understood something of this divine love are *those who have allowed God to do something for them which they couldn't do for themselves*. That is described in the Bible as being *rescue* – either from slavery in Egypt (as God did once for the Hebrews) or from slavery to sin (man's natural, fallen state). Sadly, not everyone is willing to be rescued, and God allows people to choose to reject Him.

In Part 1 of this book, I have appealed mainly to logic and scientific evidence. Scientifically, effects have causes, and the only logical explanation for Christians doing better from all diseases recorded is the influence of Jesus. That he makes a difference in healing entails that he is alive and active, unlike all religious figures and leaders who are dead.

To deny the present existence of the living Lord Jesus Christ is utterly illogical, as praying to nothing would have no effect. In another sense, there is an evidence base for the truth of Christian claims, in that there is powerful evidence for the resurrection from eyewitnesses who were willing to risk their lives to testify to what they had seen and heard. But believing *that* Jesus is alive is not in itself enough to save us and bring us into new life as a "new creation". Believing *in*

Him *includes* believing that He exists, but it means much more as well. Again, it is relational.

So is God – the Father, Son and Holy Spirit – really all-powerful? You may still need a little persuading that, having been there before, He will be there again this time for you in your distress. Yes, He is all-powerful, and one day He will right all wrongs and execute His justice perfectly. But, frankly, if He gave us all what we deserve now, none of us would be here. The fact that judgement is delayed is all from his mercy. His patience is seen in that He gives us time to repent, to turn from our wickedness and believe in Jesus, the One whom He has sent to save us from our sins.

Historians are no less rigorous than scientists in insisting that their facts should be correct. The best attested fact in ancient history is the life, death and resurrection of Jesus Christ. Entering Jerusalem for the last time, he knew what lay ahead. Joy would turn to tears in just a few short days, and those shed by his family and friends would reflect the immense suffering he was about to go through.

Cancer is widely feared as the worst possible crisis for many people. Some are healed in Jesus' name. However, *all* can be helped, the sick and the well alike, by knowing the Cross was God's way to offer us the *both* the forgiveness *and* the new life we needed but could never have earned ourselves, and we are helped as we accept what was accomplished for us in that great act of God. Whether our disease is healed or not becomes less important than whether we repent before God, our sins are forgiven by the sacrifice of Jesus Christ, and we are born of the Spirit and start and continue to live a new life as a new creation walking in Jesus' righteousness rather than depending on our own imagined "goodness"! That is the context in which the Christian understanding of divine healing must be placed.

PART TWO

"Some people never become completely human beings and really start living until they get cancer." [38]

INTRODUCTION

Up to now, we have looked at cancer as an increasing problem. Statistics don't lie, but hope is at hand as those who believe in God seem to do better from all diseases, cancer included. Furthermore, anecdotes may be "unproven" but are so numerous that overwhelmingly they point to the existence of a God who acts when His people call on Him. And with recent moves of the Holy Spirit accelerating local healing, it could be argued that there has never been a better time to get cancer.

Now that sounds glib, and there may be readers who will take offence at what I have written. Those who have lost loved ones, or are terminally ill themselves, or who simply view malignancy as a purely physical problem devoid of a spiritual dimension, with God merely a figment of others' imaginations. Equally, have I forgotten that whilst cancer death rates are falling, the year on year increase in incidence still means that more die each year from the disease? A good time to get cancer – I might as well argue that now is the time to get knocked over crossing the road! But bear with me.

Since getting ill, I have taken to reading books written by other cancer sufferers. One, both poignant and amusing in equal measure, was penned by a journalist dying from mouth cancer.[39] The others were written from a Christian persuasion and provided different insights into the present and the future. Each author was supremely brave as he presented his journey with cancer as a narrative, from diagnosis to death. I salute each one, whilst approaching the subject from a different angle. I could have waited a year or two, then outlined my story so far. Indeed, any one of the 14 million sufferers in Britain and America could do the same, but to what end? Any understanding I have been given may well apply perfectly to my situation but not to yours and there will undoubtedly be areas which haven't bothered me (yet!) but which are major issues in the lives of others.

Instead of an unfolding narrative, I intend to focus on some of the common issues arising from the disease. What I have learnt from other writers has certainly helped distil my thoughts, particularly those whose personal journeys were coming to an end. But human wisdom and experience, to my mind, is not enough. To this end, I'm indebted to three doctors and a vicar,[40, 41, 42] all of whom *in extremis* consistently pointed to the only person truly qualified to comment from an earthly viewpoint and from the divine perspective: Jesus Christ.

In each of the following chapters, I offer my own views and build on those of others in relation to issues common in cancer. But, as each chapter unfolds, the emphasis will shift back and forward from current suffering to that experienced by Jesus and the disciples, predominantly in the last week of his life. For Jesus, theory wasn't enough. He actually suffered – physically, mentally and spiritually – and His wisdom is thus both practical and experiential. This is no cold, distant person pontificating, but a compassionate Lord and Saviour who has been there and sheds tears with us. We have much to learn from Him.

Chapter Ten

SOMETHING'S NOT RIGHT

An anxious heart weighs a man down.....[43]

My kids are growing up. The youngest one has just entered her gap year, whilst the older two girls are spread between university and working in schools as an expedition coordinator. Once a year, we still just about manage to get together for a family holiday. For this, Heather and I are grateful, even if a major attraction for the youngsters is undoubtedly a "freebie". Last year, with chemotherapy looming and the future uncertain, we took off early, enjoying some Easter sunshine in the Canary Islands. By day the older generation cycled around the island while the girls interspersed academic evasion (sunbathing) with exam revision. Even without cancer, it was a refreshing break, not least for Heather; a lovely interlude.

The hotel by night provided rich fare in unlimited quantities, and there was plenty of time to chat about the future. Some time ago, I had asked an older accountant friend what, in his opinion, was the most difficult time period for parents. Twenty to twenty five, he replied – just the age two of ours have reached! Working on the principle that if you don't ask, you'll never know, I turned the subject towards marriage, and who did they think would be first? We then talked of their friends and Jess, our oldest, ventured an order of matrimony for her best mates. Idle chat and quite fun as the wine kicked in, but based on one premise: that the status quo would continue and that life was predictable.

One night, Jess was late to dinner. One of her university friends, whom we had recently met, had texted her to say that her ex-boyfriend had just been killed in a road traffic accident. So tough, and a reminder that no matter how idyllic one's current situation, serious grot can be just around the corner.

His death was dramatic and quick, but cancer usually creeps up on you. A pattern of symptoms and signs that ultimately point to an unpleasant diagnosis often starts off minimally – a slight cough here, a mole (has it changed?) there or bowels that are a little odd, perhaps put down to age. Nothing apparently to get too alarmed about, so we keep it to ourselves.

Ultimately, cancer patients tend to present for three reasons: maybe symptoms simply persist and demand an explanation, or something new turns up, and equally questions arise; the third reason, of course, is that relatives and friends become suspicious of weight loss or a cough which the patient can no longer hide or laugh off. But it is often a slow process – though we may suspect that something is not right, the status quo is so desirable in comparison to medical attention and tests which might point to a sinister fate, that delay in presenting is more often the rule than not. I was in both of the first two camps, as slightly irritating but persistent symptoms would ultimately have led to my declaring that something was not right, before bleeding – a full six months after symptoms first arose – allowed me no further procrastination.

I was just about to preach in church. Note to budding preachers: it's always good to take your bladder and bowels out of the equation before speaking, so I nipped off for some relief. Looking back, the fresh blood in the pan was God's way of getting through to me! I managed to concentrate on whatever the subject was that day, before sheepishly opening up to Heather that for some time my innards had not been quite right and now I definitely had a problem. She was a little cross – why hadn't I told her earlier, for even if I chose not to do something about my symptoms, she would have done. Fair comment, and one that others may recognise. But beyond the practical importance of dealing with the issue and no longer subconsciously ignoring what was happening was something else.

In truth, I had suspected something was wrong for some time. The bleeding merely confirmed that the writing was on the wall. As a doctor, it was obvious to me now that I had cancer until proved otherwise, but until I presented, the status quo remained untroubled. I was a doctor, not a patient and certainly not a cancer patient. Ditto for my family: blissfully unaware of anything amiss, the sky remained blue. Coming out changed everything. Suddenly, this huge grey cloud appeared from nowhere, blotting out the sun. Unwanted, unasked for and terrifying. Questions poured from the kids. What did it mean? Was this it? Would dad make our weddings and teach our kids to play tennis? Weighed down with anxiety and devastated, they rushed home, thinking I was dying. The big one had moved in; we were now a family struggling against cancer, an enemy none of us had ever dreamed would strike so soon.

The disciples would have recognised my family's predicament. Things were going well as they followed their leader who determined where they went and what they did. They knew that not everyone liked him, for when he healed a woman on the Sabbath who had been crippled for eighteen years, the synagogue ruler was indignant and told the people only to present for healing on the other six days of the week! Jesus retorted by pointing out his hypocrisy in complaining of Sabbath day working when he and others would take their animals off to water that day. *"When he said this, all his opponents were humiliated, but the people were delighted with all the wonderful things he was doing."* [44]

To the religious leaders he was a threat, but to the disciples he was both friend and Lord. They had given up everything including their families to follow him. In doing so, their close-knit group became a new family and life was good. Growing as believers, they generally didn't begrudge the hard lifestyle as the people's need was so great. For them, the status quo was practically perfect – you are doing fine, Jesus; carry on.

But storm clouds were gathering. Jesus had already let slip something odd about a third day and a prophet dying outside Jerusalem.[45] A little later, he was more specific: *Jesus took the Twelve aside and told them, "We are going up to Jerusalem, and everything that is written by the prophets about the Son of Man will be fulfilled. He will be turned over to the Gentiles. They will mock him, insult him, spit on him, flog him and kill him. On the third day he will rise again."* [46]

The disciples were hearing words they did not want to hear. What was going on? Why should this happen? Couldn't life remain as it was? OK, a little opposition meant it wasn't perfect, but it was surely loads better than Jesus being killed. And if he knew in advance that Jerusalem would be so dangerous, no problem, there was plenty to do elsewhere. Indeed, the news was so overwhelmingly bad that they couldn't cope with it; Luke went on to say: *The disciples did not understand any of this. Its meaning was hidden from them, and they did not know what he was talking about.*[47]

But even though they didn't get it, they must have known

something wasn't right. Something new and very significant was about to happen, something which would change their lives beyond any imagination or comprehension. And by now they should have realised that when Jesus told them of his movements and predicted the outcome, they needed to listen up, for his future and theirs was being spoken about. But for once his words were unwelcome and, weighed down with anxiety, they struggled to comprehend just what he was saying. Far easier to relegate any unpleasantness in the future to the back of their minds; later, they would have no choice but to understand his meaning, but for now they simply continued on their way.

Jesus alone knew where he was going and what was coming. All his earthly life had led to this point. He could have ducked out of his destiny, but that would have denied who he was. In that sense, he had no choice as his earthly ministry took him inexorably towards his crisis, the Cross.

In the early stages of cancer, patients may suspect, like the disciples, that something is wrong but be in denial. But God knows everything. Our individual situations in no way take Him unawares. Thank goodness that, "Horrors! Richard's got cancer; I didn't spot that one coming" is not part of His vocabulary. He knows the end from the beginning for each of us, and whilst we may see it as undesirable and unpleasant, it is more than comforting to know that we are not in it alone. For the future is fully under His control.

Chapter Eleven

"IT CAN'T BE TRUE"

Jesus asked the boy's father, "How long has he been like this?"

From childhood," he answered. "It has often thrown him into fire or water to kill him. But if you can do anything, take pity on us and help us."

"If you can?" said Jesus. "Everything is possible for him who believes."

Immediately the boy's father exclaimed, "I do believe; help me overcome my unbelief." [48]

Colonoscopy is an unpleasant business. Drinking a litre of laxative beforehand was just the prelude to a certain indignity as the scope delved into parts it had no right to explore. Within seconds, it had found what it was looking for as the polyp dominated the monitor, unpleasant and sinister. The team had seen it all before and I, too, was not hugely surprised as my symptoms in my age group add up to cancer. I merely kicked myself for not turning up earlier; had I done so, I might have spared myself the lymph node and saved a great deal of trouble. Even when the initial biopsy came back clear, it was an obvious red herring, later corrected when the polyp was removed *in toto*. I had cancer, the facts were clear, time to get on with it.

During my 29 years as a doctor, some patients have received malignant news in the same purely logical way as I did: *"I thought it probably was, doctor,"* and make the necessary arrangements. But for others the shock is greater because it is so unexpected. A man in his forties comes to mind. He had originally presented with what was thought to be indigestion, given treatment and asked to return if he got any worse. He did, but not for three years, by which time he had lost much weight and had a mass at the top of his abdomen, representing an advanced stomach carcinoma. A few weeks later he was dead. He had suspected that something was not right, but delayed coming my way until too late; nevertheless, learning that he had cancer, not indigestion, still came as a huge surprise.

A proportion of patients react more strongly still and break down. Often suspecting something sinister, they keep it firmly under wraps until formal diagnosis shifts it inexorably to the forefront of their lives. Denial? Well yes, but as one of their number, I can appreciate that something else is going on. Denial has a half-brother; it is called hope and all those who know deep down that their body is misbehaving cling to a hope that things will simply turn out OK in the end - that the body will right itself without a doctor's interference. Of course, it leads to delay and our minds revving into over-drive as we dare to believe that nothing major is wrong whilst at the same time doubting our instincts and pondering where we will end up.

In many ways our situations reflect that of the boy's father in the passage above. His son's life was under grave threat from epilepsy. Worried beyond belief by the many times his son had been burnt and nearly drowned, he came to Jesus with little hope and expectation and rather more doubt. Asking only for help, the possibility of cure seemed beyond him. He had probably heard of Jesus' exploits, but surely it couldn't be true that they would extend to healing his boy? That things would turn out fine? Much was going on in his head and when challenged by the Lord to grasp that *everything is possible for him who believes*, he very honestly admitted that his level of belief was poor but that more faith would be good. Jesus went on to heal the epileptic boy and the doubting was over. What his father initially saw as impossible came to pass. What could not be true took place and his situation changed forever.

This man had been used to pleading on behalf of his son. Pleading for help from others and very likely pleading with God as he questioned why such a disaster had befallen his family. Now those days were over for him, but for us as new cancer patients our time of questioning has just begun. *Surely it can't be true. Not me. Not now. Isn't this just a bad dream from which I'll wake up with the sun shining?* As our feelings kick in, a potent mix of disbelief, anger, shock and tears pour out alongside questions and concerns as we try to get to grips with the bad news. Sometimes our emotions (*it can't be true*) will be in direct conflict with our rational processing (*42% is almost a 50:50 chance*) but usually feelings win through. *It's just not fair. What's going on?* In the midst of tumult, our thoughts may turn to God; we may question His existence, His goodness and His even-handedness; and even if we grant that He is up there, somewhere, hasn't He forgotten us? And it's no good knowing that emotions can be unreliable, for they are integral to who we are. The disciples were no different.

Jesus had told them that he was going to be killed in Jerusalem, but they neither understood nor wished to understand what he was saying. Indeed, as they entered the city it was as if they had completely forgotten his words, so caught up were they in the normal business of life. *After Jesus had said this, he went on ahead, going up to*

Jerusalem. As he approached Bethphage and Bethany at the hill called the Mount of Olives, he sent two of his disciples, saying to them, "Go to the village ahead of you, and as you enter it, you will find a colt tied there, which no-one has ever ridden. Untie it and bring it here. If anyone asks you, "Why are you untying it?" tell him, "The Lord needs it." [49]

Normal life. Jesus issuing instructions and telling his followers in advance exactly what would happen. The disciples find the donkey, inform the owners what they are doing in borrowing it and then as Jesus rides into town, worship breaks out: *As he went along, people spread their cloaks along the road. When he came near the place where the road goes down the Mount of Olives, the whole crowd of disciples began joyfully to praise God in loud voices for all the miracles they had seen....* [50]

The disciples were happy. Welcomed into town, their Master feted on a donkey and the people on their side. What could be better? No clouds in their sky, and any memory of his warnings would have been quickly counteracted by the thought that no harm could possibly take place to him here. He was among friends and life was sweet. Their belief, their trust, was in the present, but it was about to be shattered.

The Pharisees told Jesus to rebuke his disciples for the noise they were making in worship. He refused, and then upset the religious authorities further by driving out those selling in the temple and by answering with authority those who questioned his authority. He continued to teach *... and all the people came early in the morning to hear him at the temple.* [51] Afraid of the people, the religious leaders needed to stop Jesus in his tracks when the crowds were absent. Figuring the best way to do so was by an inside job, they turned to a disaffected disciple, Judas, for help. The opportunity arose at the end of the Last Supper, a time when the disciples' disbelief and dismay over the way events were shaping was clear. Matthew records:

Then Jesus told them, "This very night you will all fall away on account of me, for it is written:

> *"'I will strike at the shepherd,*
> *and the sheep of the flock*
> *will be scattered.'*

But after I have risen, I will go ahead of you into Galilee."
Peter replied, "Even if all fall away on account of you, I never will."
"I tell you the truth," Jesus answered, "this very night, before the cock crows, you will disown me three times."
But Peter declared, "Even if I have to die with you, I will never disown you." And all the other disciples said the same.[52]

The disciples once again were wrestling with what their ears were telling them. Not only would losing their leader turn their world upside down, but they themselves would be shown up in the process. Not a comforting prospect and testosterone kicked in as egos, notably Peter's, refused to accept their Master's word. Emotions ran high as they declined to believe a man whose word had never proved false before. It was not that they doubted him; but in demonstrating their solidarity, they couldn't see that the abrupt change in circumstances would affect them to such an extent that their behaviour would become unrecognisable. Even if disaster struck and Jesus was gone, surely it couldn't be true that without him and in danger, they would turn from men of faith to abject and weak liars?

They would, and yet Jesus didn't condemn them. He not only predicted Peter's denial, but made arrangements, post-Resurrection, to meet up with them all in Galilee. Whilst saddened to the point of tears, he wasn't fazed by their doubts, their weakness and ultimate failure at crisis time. Many of his men had been tough fishermen, and now they had three years' first-hand experience of God on earth; but in dire straits even they would fail to pass muster. He knew it and still loved them.

Just like us, the disciples would discover that it *was* true. It was not maybe what they had hoped for, and only later would they understand the bigger picture: that Jesus had to die and that God would always be with them, no matter how bad the circumstances. As the big one turns up without fanfare to threaten our lives, God understands all our questions. He knows what we are going through. Two thousand years ago He proved that was the case and that includes the most angst-ridden question of all.

Chapter Twelve

WHY ME?

The word of the LORD came to me, saying,

> *"Before I formed you in the*
> *womb I knew you,*
> *before you were born I set you apart;*
> *I appointed you as a prophet*
> *to the nations."*

"Ah, Sovereign LORD." I said, "I do not know how to speak: I am only a child."

But the LORD said to me, "Do not say, 'I am only a child.' You must go to everyone I send you to and say whatever I command you. Do not be afraid of them, for I am with you and will rescue you," declares the LORD. [53]

It seems that reality TV shows are the vogue on both sides of the Atlantic these days. Contestants may sing, act or even get their dogs to perform in the interests of fame. All have one goal in mind – to become the chosen one. If successful, their being chosen will change their lives for the better – or so they hope, for in reality it is a highly competitive business providing only a small chance of success. Nevertheless, wide-eyed, they present themselves and their talent: *Here I am, choose me* and await the judges' verdict.

Cancer is different! Even if we are not aware of the appalling statistics nowadays, most people appreciate that developing the disease is at the very least a risk, but one that in all honesty they would rather not befall them. So we whisper the word quietly. Now is not the time for fanfare, and rather than raising our head above the parapet in the manner of performers, we lie low, keeping our heads down, hoping that we will go unnoticed and that the disease will pass us by. Or we take a more active approach, centred on leading a good life or eating healthily and going down the gym once in a while. Maybe that will keep us safe. And then, boom, the disease strikes, mercilessly and unpredictably, dashing our hopes forever. And we wonder, *Why me?*

Jeremiah certainly did. Given a top job by God, he was initially reluctant, using his age as an excuse. The unspoken implication was this: why me? Can't you give the job to someone else? Someone a bit older and more capable perhaps? But God knows what He is doing, and in selecting the young boy for this role, He spelt out future realities: Jeremiah would win no popularity contests and would make many enemies, none of whom he should fear, for his God would be with him throughout, and that was what mattered. Nevertheless, I guess that what was put on the table that day was less than tempting. Only Jeremiah's obedience would overcome his natural reticence, but he would discover that God would prove true to His Word.

Jeremiah must have wondered why God chose him for such a thankless role. We too may wonder why cancer has come our way. God clearly had His reasons for choosing the young lad and, if we are honest, sometimes there are obvious clues to why cancer has developed in our bodies. John Diamond, a journalist who developed mouth cancer, was told by some well-meaning friends that it wasn't his fault. Ruthlessly honest, he dismissed their concerns for his mental well-being. A lifelong smoker, he knew why he had been afflicted. Equally, processed red meat is linked with bowel cancer. I have always loved sausages and pork pies.... But often there is no clear reason and no fault can be attached. My younger sister is currently in remission following treatment for myeloma. This is a disease with no known cause and is currently incurable. Breast cancer is another case in point. Hugely common, its main risk factor is simply being female. Prostate cancer similarly afflicts many men for no good reason, but regardless of whether or not we have had any influence in causing the disease, the question remains, *Why me, not him or her?* So let's grapple with this big one and come to terms with it, for only then can we move beyond it and respond to picking up such an unwanted present.

Logically, we know that approximately 42% on both sides of the Atlantic get cancer. That is plenty, but not as high as the 58% who get away with it. We may think of it as two clubs, but only one has free entry. The other comes at a cost, but again why should I have to pay? We can all recall those who have smoked all their lives and got away Scot-free. Others, with an aversion to exercise and who wouldn't jog if their lives were threatened, also saunter on, untroubled by the ogre.

And it seems if not unfair, just not very fair. But inspiringly, some people in extreme adversity seem to view their situation from exactly the opposite perspective. *Why me? – Well, why not?* I came across one beautifully written example and include it as an encouragement for those with cancer who grapple with this very question. Rob Bewley is a priest in the Midlands. His wife, Rosie, developed an aggressive brain tumour in 2006 which took her speech, her mobility, her independence and then her life the next year, aged forty-one.

In answering the question, "Where is God when it hurts?", he wrote this on behalf of Rosie:

I genuinely believe that through her terminal illness, she drew not away from God but closer to Him. Although she, at times, grew frustrated with her increasing disability, she remarkably never became bitter, responding to those who lamented that this shouldn't happen to someone as lovely as her with, "Well, who should it happen to, then?"

Rob continued, *As the disease progressively robbed her of her ability to communicate with me and with her friends, it could not steal from her her ability to communicate with her heavenly Father, and she spent increasing amounts of time in silent prayer and study of God's Word. She lived through her illness as one who, if she was not to be healed, knew exactly where she was going. I had the painful privilege of being by her side at the end of her earthly life. She had been unconscious with her eyes closed for five days, but surrounded by friends, her eyes opened wide and she stared straight ahead for a minute or so. Then she simply stopped breathing. I believe she was given a taste of the glory to which she was heading.*[54]

Rosie and others, in turning the question around, have come up with the best answer possible to this conundrum. Nobody ever said life was fair, and whether or not we contribute to our malignancy through inadvisable lifestyles, the fact is that within a cohort of like individuals, only some will get the big C. That's life and we know it.

Jesus could have asked exactly the same question. *Why me?* And it was even worse for him for he knew what was coming; leaving heaven for earth would be no picnic and he could hardly have relished it. But he knew that his Father's choice was immaculate, for the sacrificial lamb had to be both man and God and there was only one fit for this purpose. Like Jeremiah, he had a role which only he could play and, in our own calamity, we too are in position with no substitutes allowed.

Rosie turned the question around and Jesus fully understood why *him*. But *why me?* is such a heart-wrenching question that, without a satisfactory answer, what begins as a sense of unfairness may progress to deep unhappiness and bitterness if prolonged. I think Rosie has much to teach us here. For what is reasonable as an initial response to cancer becomes not only unhelpful but actually the wrong question. A far better one is this: *What can I learn from my disease*, or even, *what is God teaching me through all this ghastliness?* For just as Rosie gained a lot in the last year of her life by turning a negative into a positive, others, whatever their life expectancy, can do the same.

Why me? It's not fair that I've got cancer when others haven't. That's not how Rosie saw it. *I'm too young, still in the prime of life and too vibrant and good looking to be brought down by the disease.* So was Rosie, but it didn't stop her being affected. Instead, her faith helped her to deal with the catastrophe that had come her way. She saw through foolish suggestions that she was too attractive or had more right than anyone else to remain untouched by evil. Her response was both faithful and practical – and in responding like that, in the short time left to her, life had both meaning and purpose.

Chapter Thirteen

STOP WORK? I'M TOO BUSY!

As Jesus and the disciples were on their way, he came to a village where a woman named Martha opened her home to him. She had a sister called Mary, who sat at the Lord's feet listening to what he said. But Martha was distracted by all the preparations that had to be made. She came to him and asked, "Lord, don't you care that my sister has left me to do the work by myself? Tell her to help me!"

"Martha, Martha," the Lord answered, "you are worried and upset about many things, but only one thing is needed. Mary has chosen what is better, and it will not be taken away from her." [55]

Martha is famed as a classic workaholic. It may well be that her sister worked just as hard as she did generally, but only Mary seemed able to take time off where appropriate. And Martha resented it, not silently but publicly complaining to Jesus that her sister's actions led to her needing to work even harder. If we are honest, most of us will appreciate her dilemma. Hospitality was highly valued, and when the Lord of the Universe turns up at your door, the stakes are raised somewhat! Martha was a hard worker all right, but had lost the bigger picture that her sister had grasped. Two thousand years on, not much has changed.

As a junior doctor, it was taken as read that you pulled your weight. Skiving was unthinkable and even taking a day off for genuine illness meant that your over-pressed colleagues would not thank you. Once, I picked up a vomiting bug and was forced to miss three days' work; even the loss of half a stone did not save me from the repercussions! The only other time I had missed a day's work through illness was after a game of football on Christmas Day, 1990. We were working in Tanzania and I relaxed by playing up front for the village team. With our best player alongside me and drawing the attentions of most of the defenders, I was not only visible as the only white man around but given ample opportunities to score. That particular day, Stuarti played the ball through for me to shoot, but as I lifted my foot, a spectator rushed through the goal. With no defender near and just the keeper to beat, I had not expected the illicit tackle and fell awkwardly, breaking my collarbone. Two days later, dominant arm in a sling and in a little discomfort, hospital life for me returned to normal.

I mention my working history merely to illustrate how motivated people dislike being off work due to illness. I see examples regularly in general practice; people present with symptoms that fully justify some time off, but I practically have to talk them into it. I am not speaking here of broken legs in manual workers. Their sick note is mandatory. It is more those who work overlong hours and become stressed, anxious or depressed as a result. Eventually we come to an agreement, based on what is best for them in the long term.

Pre-retirement, most peoples' lives are dominated by work, whether paid or unpaid. Having worked at Papworth (cardiothoracic) Hospital in my younger days, I was intrigued by a comment made by a more experienced surgeon who had worked in the same hospital, long after I had left. Dying from leukaemia, he admitted that his identity had become tied in with his job. Cancer made him rethink, but even then, and how true this is for so many of us, being forced to stop work was both freeing and devastating.

And it is not something you can plan. Like having a baby, there is no perfect time to get cancer. It is no respecter of schedule, not usually turning up between jobs, whilst on sabbatical or during an elderly gap year. And even if it did, our busy lives would still render it most inconvenient. Turning up unannounced on the doorstep, it enters our lives at a time of its own choosing and we need to make the best of it. If it is not too serious, we may be able to carry on working, at least through part of our treatment. One of our practice secretaries developed breast cancer and worked half days throughout her period of radiotherapy. I took time off for surgery, radio and chemotherapy, but then returned to work normally for a couple of months before more major chemotherapy again sidelined me. Others, despite their continuing intentions, are too sick ever to work again. And it is hard.

Loss comes in many forms. Malignancy specialises in causing physical loss but doesn't sniff at mental incapacitation and damage to relationships. But loss of working identity is a particularly nasty side effect of the disease. Granted, we may have invested too much of ourselves in work, and many of us might benefit from slowing down, but to have our role as breadwinner or mum running a home taken away abruptly, with no time to wind down, is a form of bereavement. Retirement lay ahead, and would be nice one day but not now.

Were the disciples in a similar boat? Jesus' ministry was nothing short of sensational and their working identity as followers was intimately engaged with his. Three years in, they were still pretty green and would have envisaged a long road ahead before being cut loose. They were not ready for his exit; all he had to do was avoid Jerusalem.... But the

Father had a different plan. He knew what His Son was doing on earth and how much remained to be done, but for Jesus there was not to be the sort of retirement the modern mind anticipates. For just as some with cancer never reach standard retirement age, neither did Jesus. From our perspective, Jesus' earthly ministry seems to have been relatively short.

But mankind needed something more than the teaching and miracles, important as they were. The problem of sin, and mankind's separation from the Father, was so serious that Jesus' work included something that the disciples had done their best to ignore. He had told them that he only did what he saw the Father doing, and that of himself he could do nothing. He was completely subject to his heavenly Father, and knew that one day his job on earth would end as it did, at the Father's behest. As he entered Jerusalem, the time had come.

Even though Jesus knew that this was it – the end of his working life on earth – to say that it still came as a shock is something of an understatement. Although his ministry had lasted but three short years, he had poured everything he had into it. His arrest would not only provide a stark end to all that he had built up through work, but would lead very rapidly to an appalling death. In anguish, with an unjust trial ahead.

He withdrew about a stone's throw beyond them, knelt down and prayed, "Father, if you are willing, take this cup from me; yet not my will, but yours be done." An angel from heaven appeared to him and strengthened him. And being in anguish, he prayed more earnestly, and his sweat was like drops of blood falling to the ground. [56]

When we think of suffering, pain and forced early retirement from familiar work in the cancer sufferer, it may help to remember that Jesus was no stranger to any of these. Having shared our humanity, he knows the pains we go through as he felt pain just as we do.

Did the Cross take place at a convenient time, allowing adequate preparation and everything neatly in place for his subordinates? The Bible does not tell us that! It does make it clear that Jesus agreed to endure the Cross because he knew the Father had a particular plan in mind. He still had a job to do, but one which was very different from what had taken place before. His new role was the Father's decision and Jesus willingly endured it, knowing the bigger picture and how much was at stake. For Jesus, everything changed, and in our sufferings we need to know that it was all for us.

When cancer supervenes, sometimes this means the end of our working lives, but could it be that something better lies ahead? Whether our time is short or we are given more years, Jesus' saving death and life means there is the opportunity to relate to him – not only for our remaining time here but for all eternity. To do so is a decision we need to make, and at the end of this book there is a prayer you could use to begin on that path. It is not too late to do so.

Whether or not return to work is possible, life, as my secretary reminded me after her treatment and my diagnosis, will never be the same again. But why assume that it is all downhill from here on – that loss of full-time work, status or salary is a cast iron negative that will continue until death? As all three drift out of reach, leaving behind a sense of loss that may be overpowering, could it be that this time of change may throw up possibilities which you had never dreamed of and which more than counteract the downsides? One of my favourite Bible verses promises this:

"For I know the plans I have for you," declares the
LORD, "plans to prosper you and not to harm you, plans

to give you hope and a future. Then you will call upon me and come and pray to me, and I will listen to you. You will seek me and find me when you seek me with all your heart. I will be found by you," declares the LORD, "and will bring you back from captivity...." [57]

The context was a letter from the prophet Jeremiah to the Israelites, who were exiled for their disobedience to God. Their biggest problem was captivity. We may consider that ours is cancer, although, like the Israelites, if we lack the right relationship with God that may be an even bigger problem.

The principle stands that the Lord has good plans for our lives and our futures. Our job is to seek Him with all our heart. We may never fully understand why God has allowed us to develop cancer. But there is one thing to which I can abundantly testify: any plan from God is far superior to even the best of our own plans. Our reduced circumstances provide an opportunity for us to look to God, who can show us a new and better way forward, one that we will never regret. Just as life may appear to be ending, a new chapter is within our grasp. All we have to do is ask Him.

Chapter Fourteen

I FEEL SO ALONE

*... And the word of the L*ORD *came to him: "What are you doing here, Elijah?"*

*He replied, "I have been very zealous for the L*ORD *God Almighty. The Israelites have rejected your covenant, broken down your altars, and put your prophets to death with the sword. I am the only one left, and now they are trying to kill me too."* [58]

The prophet Elijah had just scaled the summit of his career. He had arranged to meet the 450 idolatrous prophets of Baal on Mount Carmel to prove once and for all whose was the true god. Sacrificing a bull each, the challenge was for each deity to spontaneously consume the meat by fire sent from above. Of course, Baal proved impotent whereas the God of Israel sent sufficient fire not only to burn up the meat but also the wood, stones and soil, despite Elijah having drenched the sacrifice three times using four large jars of water. And not only did God provide a *tour de force* in response to Elijah's faith, He then emphasised His approval by sending rain, thus ending a three year drought. No wonder Elijah ran from the mountain like the wind; he was delighted to have survived the ordeal, and also no doubt wished to avoid a serious soaking.

God was with him and his work could not have been

going better. But this all time high would not last. His sworn enemy, Queen Jezebel, sent a message promising to deal with him as he had dealt with the false prophets of Baal. With a price on his head, once again he ran, this time for his life. Arriving in the desert, he sat down under a broom tree and prayed that he might die. Strengthened by an angel who fed and watered him, he then travelled for forty days to a particular cave where God had a word with him. *What are you up to, Elijah?* In reply, he reminded God of all His prophets that Jezebel and the wicked King Ahab had put to death, and that he alone was left.

He alone? Actually, he wasn't, for the Lord would remind him that there remained 7,000 in Israel who had also not bowed the knee to Baal. And his perception that there was no-one to help him would also prove inaccurate for God had in mind a successor, Elisha, who would follow him as an attendant until the time was right to take his place as prophet. His working days almost over, it was the end of the line for Elijah, but what a finale! Taken up to heaven in a whirlwind, it was time for the next man to step up to the plate.

Elijah had received very bad news, news which applied to him and no-one else. Feeling all alone, he almost capitulated until God strengthened him through the angel and through a direct word.

A diagnosis of cancer is shattering too, and we too may feel very alone. With my doctor's hat on, wherever possible I tend to ask for relatives to be present whenever I supply bad news, for patients may understandably go blank and remember little afterwards. As a patient suspecting the worst and even with my medical background, I was still very grateful for Heather's accompanying me to the surgeon's office for my biopsy result. We had always shared problems and this was no time to change. But, as treatment started, I was on my own. After she had kissed me goodbye and poignantly taken possession of my wedding ring, I entered the operating theatre alone. Neither was Heather welcome to share the X-rays bombarding me every weekday in the early part of that year, and going halves with chemotherapy also wasn't an option! These joys and any repercussions were mine and mine alone.

That is not to say that relatives are unaffected by the disease. Far from it; in many ways, cancer is worse for those watching their loved ones suffer. Thus far, I have shed no tears, but my girls have. Cancer is a family affair, and none of us will remain unchanged by it. That said, it is still ultimately my problem, not theirs; my life, subject to my final decisions, and if stuff goes wrong, I pick up the pieces.

Reading around the subject, many people have found cancer to be quite a lonely experience. They may be surrounded by well-wishers offering a variety of opinions and solutions but all from the outside, looking in. Some will draw closer to you at this time; they are to be cherished. Others will shy away, unable to cope with the reality of their friend's predicament. Such estrangement acts subconsciously as a betrayal of friendship at a time when it is needed most. But with or without their support, we enter a place we have never visited before, alone, and it is scary.

Jesus never had cancer but, as we have seen, knew extreme anguish, pain – and rejection from those he'd been close to. That makes him well qualified to speak into our lonely situation today.

But wasn't he surrounded by loyal friends who were with him to the end, guys he had met up with again after a short interlude? Not according to God's Word. After being betrayed by one of his closest friends, Jesus was seized and taken to the high priest.

... Peter followed at a distance. But when they had kindled a fire in the middle of the courtyard and had sat

down together, Peter sat down with them. A servant girl saw him seated there in the firelight. She looked closely at him and said, "This man was with him."

But he denied it. "Woman, I don't know him," he said.

A little later someone else saw him and said, "You also are one of them."

"Man, I am not," Peter replied.

About an hour later another asserted, "Certainly this fellow was with him, for he is a Galilean."

Peter replied, "Man, I don't know what you're talking about!" Just as he was speaking, the cock crowed. The Lord turned and looked straight at Peter....[59]

Betrayal by a disciple turned enemy was bad enough, but such disloyalty and lack of solidarity from one of his closest and toughest colleagues must have been heart-breaking for Jesus, even though he knew it was coming. And the others were nowhere to be seen. All he had taught them, all they had been through together, seemed to count for nothing now. He was on his own, and his friends disappearing was just the start. As the authorities began to flex their muscles, the crowd turned on him. Given an obvious choice between selecting a notorious murderer or an unblemished miracle-worker, they unthinkably chose the latter to die. As the beating began and the end of his life on earth loomed, all that Jesus had left to lose was his clothes, bartered for by sneering soldiers.

The Cross was both the pinnacle of agony and an extremely lonely place. As an instrument of torture it was un-matched and indeed a few centuries later it would be banned for being too extreme. Many people with cancer suffer pain, sometimes literally excruciatingly, and not always fully relieved by medication or other treatments. Fortunately, in the last couple of days before death, pain tends to ease off, and many are observed to be calmer and more peaceful, ready for the next phase. Tremendously comforting for them as well as for suffering relatives, it was not a comfort afforded to Jesus in his final hours. For him, the agony would have ratcheted up minute by minute until his body could take it no more. And his suffering was magnified by loneliness.

Now that is odd, for during those six long hours on the tree his mother, her sister and two other ladies were there supporting him, allowing Jesus to ensure that Mary would be looked after subsequently. He also had a brief conversation with the two criminals crucified either side of him, one of whom believed in him. So even though the bulk of his followers had fluffed their chance to show allegiance at this most crucial of times, he was not physically totally alone.

His sense of utter isolation came from separation from his Father. As he bore our sins on the tree, the Father turned His back, temporarily shunning His own beloved Son. Recording the words, *"Eloi, Eloi, lama sabachthani?"*[60] Matthew tells us of Jesus' spiritual agony as for the first time in his life he was truly alone. Forsaken by mankind and heaven, and all for our sakes, his misery can only be imagined.

Jesus endured that temporary isolation from his Father so that we need not be separated (by our sins) from God forever. Our bodies may fail us and friends and family let us down, but even as we come to the end of the road, God is still there, beckoning us to Him.

We have an opportunity to end our separation from the Father by repenting and turning to Jesus, accepting that only his goodness and his sacrifice can save us on the day of Judgement. Lonely with cancer? There's no need. While there is still time, why not call out to Him?

Chapter Fifteen

MAYBE IT WILL BE OK?

But the Israelites went through the sea on dry ground, with a wall of water on their right and on their left. That day the LORD saved Israel from the hands of the Egyptians, and Israel saw the Egyptians lying dead on the shore. And when the Israelites saw the great power the LORD displayed against the Egyptians, the people feared the LORD and put their trust in Him and in Moses his servant.[61]

The Bible is full of examples where God came through unexpectedly but decisively at crunch time. The parting of the Red Sea was certainly that. Had he failed to rescue them, His people faced being slaughtered in vast numbers. Seeing their enemies in chariots on the horizon must have been truly terrifying for the Israelites, but God is always faithful and when the rubber hit the road He performed the unexpected with aplomb. And His people were not the only ones to experience His power. With hardened hearts, the Egyptians pursued their defenceless prey, only for the angel of God and the pillar of cloud to move from in front of the Israelites to behind them, bringing light to them but darkness to their pursuers. The Lord then threw the Egyptian army into confusion, causing the wheels of their chariots to come off. At this point the Egyptian horsemen knew the

game was up, saying, *"Let's get away from the Israelites!
The Lord is fighting for them against Egypt"* but by now
it was too late. Moses stretched his hand back over the sea
and it flowed back, covering the entire army of Pharaoh. *Not
one of them survived.*

Throughout their flight from captivity to the Red Sea, the
Israelites, and their leader Moses in particular, must have
wondered whether they would be OK. Seeing their enemy
bearing down on them would only have intensified their
concerns and *they were terrified and cried out to the Lord.*
In fact, things were so bad that they wished they had stayed
put, saying, *"... It would have been better for us to serve
the Egyptians than to die in the desert!"*

*Moses answered the people, "Do not be afraid. Stand
firm and you will see the deliverance the Lord will bring
you today. The Egyptians you see today you will never see
again. The Lord will fight for you; you need only to be
still."* [62]

And so it proved, but not before much heart-searching and
fear had gripped the people. Not knowing as a nation whether
they would see another day, the people had no choice but to
depend on God, and after seeing His display of power, we
are told *the people feared the Lord and put their trust in
Him and in Moses His servant.* How couldn't they?

We may never be faced with such a dramatic need for
God to act right here, right now, but life throws up plenty
of opportunities for us to seek His help – especially (but not
only of course) where situations are going badly and there
is little, if anything, that we can do about it; where being
OK depends more on Him than us. As I wrote this, the kids'
hard work was being tested as they sat school and university
exams. It did not go entirely smoothly, with at least one
question misread and poorly answered, but a chance to make
up marks the following week. Futures hang in the balance,

but they all worked hard and at least tried to do their best. It takes me back to my schooldays when two of my exams had gone badly, putting my place in medical school under threat. The papers had gone in, two months for results, what could I do? And would I (and will they) be OK? Crunch time!

Developing cancer, in some ways, reminds me of my student days. Instead of presenting our minds for examination, our bodies are offered up instead. How will we fare? A good chance of cure might be likened to a pass, with complete cure almost certainly a distinction! But, for others, the exam might be too hard and only palliative care possible. As we take the tests, the outcome remains in the balance.

When I was a lad, school exams were a one-off. I remember one chap from the year above who dropped down to our year, but he was very much the exception. Nowadays, schools in the UK adopt retakes as the norm where results have not quite gone to plan; better grades sometimes follow, although I am personally so glad that this option was not available in my day; one exam was quite bad enough, thanks, with no guarantee of an improvement second time around.

But as we approach the results of important cancer tests, we cannot hope to improve things of our own volition. Trying a bit harder next time, or getting ourselves in better shape does not apply. There is no next time, only the present counts. Passing or failing remains in the hands of others, and we await their deliberations. And the result does not simply allow progression into university or the job market, both of which are optional. Instead, it has a say on our very existence on earth.

The disciples' future also lay in the balance. They had just seen their master carried down from the Cross and laid in a tomb. He had promised so much. Such a pity. Game over, and what would become of them? Peter had already been spotted as a Galilean. The rest, too, were easily identifiable and hugely at risk. How did they respond, these hitherto brave men of God:

On the evening of that first day of the week, when the disciples were together, with the doors locked for fear of the Jews....

Just then, things were most definitely not OK, but...

Jesus came and stood among them and said, "Peace be with you!" After he said this, he showed them his hands and side. The disciples were overjoyed when they saw the Lord.[63]

Two thousand years on, we know the story well and expect the happy ending. But the disciples had spent days in fearful misery, hiding for their lives and seemingly forgetful of his promise to return. But return he did, never to leave them again. They may have failed their exam; he never failed.

Cancer patients awaiting the results of investigations can take heart here. Scared of the present? The future unknown? Of what may or may not lie ahead? But it needn't stay like that. The Lord of the disciples can become our Lord.

God is our refuge and strength,
an ever-present help in trouble.[64]

Seeing the resurrected Lord, all their doubts and fears were swept away as they picked themselves off the floor. The next phase in their lives would be hugely exciting but not always easy. Troubles aplenty would follow them and many would lose their lives for the sake of the gospel, but they knew that whatever happened, because of Jesus they would ultimately be OK.

Chapter Sixteen

MAYBE IT WON'T

While they were stoning him, Stephen prayed, "Lord Jesus, receive my spirit." Then he fell on his knees and cried out, "Lord, do not hold this sin against them." When he had said this, he fell asleep.[65]

Stephen was the first Christian martyr. His bravery defies belief, and his relationship with God did not prevent him from suffering and dying. One day, I look forward to humbly asking him how he had the courage not to wimp out. I suspect the answer's in the passage – he had seen *... heaven open and the Son of Man standing at the right hand of God.*[66] Given a picture of the future, nothing in the present compared to what he envisaged. That is worth holding onto as the present is indeed slipping away.

All of us beyond a certain age can think of people who have died of cancer. My own experience combines family, friends, those from church and work. My grandmother died from ovarian cancer, Heather's father from an abdominal carcinoid tumour, and her uncle and aunt also from metastatic cancer. I can think of church members I have known succumb to cancer of the rectum and gall-bladder, and a surgical boss of mine go down with myeloma. As I have mentioned many times, cancer is frequent, nasty and no respecter of status. And prayer does not always save you.

Greg was a delightful man who came to see me with a cough. A keen golfer sporting a decent tan, he looked the picture of health. But he had lost a little weight, the cough had persisted and he had smoked when younger. X-ray and CT scans confirmed the worst. Greg was a Christian, and usually when he attended my surgery we would pray about his lung tumour. But it continued to grow, despite our medical and spiritual best efforts, which included his wife and him following my advice by taking a trip to a Welsh house of prayer, Ffald-y-Brenin, which they really valued. But it failed to rescue him. A few months before he died, he bounced in to tell me of his best ever round of golf, something that left us both ridiculously pleased; but in truth we knew he was dying, and that God had chosen not to prolong his life on this earth beyond his mid-fifties. Greg was one of life's real gentlemen; my vicar, Pat, would speak at his funeral of his genuine regret at not having met him sooner.

Why did Greg die? Or two teenage boys with sarcoma? Or Malcolm, a doctor turned vicar...? No shortage of personal faith in any of these characters, or of intercessory prayers from others. But die they did, cancer victims all. Many people would regard these as prayer "failures" causing them to examine and in some instances lose their faith. Why didn't God heal X or Y? Ignoring His saving work in others, they lay any shortcomings at His door, pronounce themselves dissatisfied and walk away. What they are essentially saying is that unless you do things my way, God, with my agenda and timescale to the fore, then either you don't care or you aren't there.

Could I gently challenge this attitude. My intention is not to criticise but to redirect thinking from that which is common, but unhelpful and inaccurate, towards something not only more useful, but which practically applies to what we see today. I refer back to testing times for the disciples:

Now Thomas (called Didymus), one of the Twelve, was not with the disciples when Jesus came. So the other disciples told him, "We have seen the Lord!"

But he said to them, "Unless I see the nail marks in his hands and put my finger where the nails were, and put my hand into his side, I will not believe it."

A week later his disciples were in the house again, and Thomas was with them. Though the doors were locked, Jesus came and stood among them and said, "Peace be with you!" Then he said to Thomas, "Put your finger here; see my hands. Reach out your hand and put it in my side. Stop doubting and believe."

Thomas said to him, "My Lord and my God!"

Then Jesus told him, "Because you have seen me, you have believed; blessed are those who have not seen and yet have believed." [67]

Thomas wanted things his way. We refer to him as "doubting Thomas", and Jesus commanded him to stop doubting. Doubt is never commended in Scripture, though many modern preachers ignore that fact, wrongly asserting that doubt is part of faith! Jesus certainly didn't teach that. He had revealed himself physically to the others and Thomas had missed out. Now the apostle dug his feet in, making it clear that no matter how convincing his friends' accounts were, no way was he going to believe in the resurrection without first-hand evidence. *"Unless I see ... I will not believe."* That "unless", setting up a condition, makes it sound as though Thomas was determined events should turn out *his* way. Jesus at this point could have simply walked away from Thomas, but graciously he didn't, instead offering him the physical evidence he craved. But Jesus' offer came with a warning. ***Stop doubting and believe.***

Thomas was one of hundreds of people who saw the risen Jesus before his ascension. The testimony of these eyewitnesses would be crucial in proclaiming that Jesus was alive, but he shared with the disciples a great truth: it was good that they believed, but they had had an advantage in actually seeing the resurrected Son of God face to face. How much greater the blessing that awaited those who would not see his physical body on earth yet who resolutely believed in him.

Thomas's mistake was not to accept what he had been told by people he should have trusted. Determined to pursue his own course, he insisted on making Jesus pass through a set of hoops before he was prepared to believe him. Kindly, Jesus acceded to his request on that occasion. But Thomas had been foolish. Today, many people treat God in a similar fashion. For them to believe in His Son, He must fulfil certain criteria of *their* choosing, be of a particular character suiting *them* and, above all, must not make them feel uncomfortable in any way.

A lady I met on the beach opposite my house comes to mind. She was sitting, gazing out to sea. The tide was in, and as I walked the dog backwards and forwards along the shoreline, I would pass in front of her every few minutes. It would have been rude not to stop and chat, so I did. It turned out that she was staying with one of my neighbours and loved travelling. Discovering that I did too, she asked me why East Africa was such a common destination, and learnt that Christian mission tended to be responsible. She then opened up, giving me her views on faith, God and existence. But it soon transpired that her faith was concocted: cherry-picking favoured bits from Christianity, she then added in personal beliefs and extracts from other faiths in order to counteract Christian "stuff" that was unacceptable to her. Like the virgin birth, Jesus being not just a good man but God and our only

Saviour from sin; the bodily resurrection of Jesus, and his being the Judge of all mankind at a real Judgment – because all those beliefs are exclusive to Christianity and conflict with the claims of other faiths. When pushed, the nub of the issue for her was that the life of Jesus Christ demands a response, one that she was not prepared to give. Adamant that she would not believe in the God of the Bible, she instead preferred one whom she thought she could tailor to her own opinions and desires.

Such a view is sadly common – and leaves the holder not only stuck on a fence but profoundly unsatisfied as, year on year, thoughts circle with no resolution. Like Thomas, the lady on the beach wanted things done her way. Unlike Thomas, so far she has not changed her position. So where does that leave us? Do we, too, make up our own religion, based on our own feelings, opinions and theories, or do we choose to trust in the true God who has told us all we need to know about Himself, who healed miraculously in biblical times and who (on both the statistical and anecdotal evidence cited in this book) still does so today? Put this way, the choice appears a no-brainer, but I am aware that many people still walk away from this all-powerful God who has revealed Himself – because they have become discouraged.

In reporting Koenig's statistics, neither he nor I have hidden what is revealed by a cursory look, namely that whilst health overall is undoubtedly significantly improved by faith, not all papers were positive. On average, one-fifth were either neutral (mainly) or, occasionally, negative. Equally, none of the healing evangelists profiled in chapter 8 ever claims that *everyone* prayed for is healed. Only Jesus, as far as our data indicates, had a 100% success rate. Why should that be? Isn't that rather disappointing? Doesn't it make prayer for healing rather "hit or miss"? And why bother if the answer may be "no"? Because it might be YES! One of the evangelists, Reinhard Bonnke, has extensive experience of God's healing power. If anyone could fully understand this mysterious business it would be him. But Reinhard doesn't understand, and humbly continues to pray for people through obedience to God's Word, not because he fully comprehends the process. He recognises that sometimes people get healed and sometimes they don't – that faith is crucial somewhere in the process, and if someone is not healed, no blame must be attached. This point is crucial, as we seek to understand why Jesus could *always* heal but we suffer some disappointments along the way.

Why did Jesus always get it right? How was this possible for him? Grasp this one and discouragement in prayer for healing should take a decisive hit. The subject is vast, but can be distilled into two main strands. Firstly, Jesus is God, while we remain affected by the Fall. The healing in Jesus' name that we see today is a foretaste of a future in which there will be no more sickness. But until Jesus comes again, Satan will continue to cause suffering and disease, and the Kingdom of God is only partially manifested on earth.

Secondly, and here is the good news, despite mankind's various follies, throughout history God has never left His people to get on with it alone. The Israelites may have had to experience slavery in exile, and we may suffer diseases like cancer, but He is always there, watching over the greatest aspect of His Creation. And we know that when we turn back to Him in prayer He listens, but always does what is right in His eyes in each and every situation. Jesus was perfectly in touch with his Father and only did what he saw his Father doing. He therefore knew whom God intended to heal, and thus had a perfect "success rate". As fallible men and women, our success rate is lower because we do not see perfectly into the mind of God. But don't let this put us off. Don't be discouraged! There are very good scriptural reasons for ministering for healing, even when we are considering doing so for the first time or maybe haven't seen results before.

God is into healing. In the psalms, David declares,

> *Praise the LORD, O my soul;*
> *all my inmost being, praise his holy name.*
> *Praise the LORD, O my soul,*
> *and forget not all his benefits –*
> *who forgives all your sins*
> *and heals all your diseases....*[68]

Jesus told his disciples explicitly to heal the sick and raise the dead, while James continued the theme later, writing to believers:

> *Is any one of you sick? He should call the elders of the church to pray over him and anoint him with oil in the name of the Lord. And the prayer offered in faith will make the sick person well; the Lord will raise him up....*[69]

We are clearly exhorted to pray over the sick, with cancer no exception, but we live in a fallen, imperfect world in which not all prayers are answered in exactly the way we would wish. God does intervene, amazingly and frequently, but not always our way. Many times He has saved me from disaster by not answering the wrong request, as I would discover only years later! But equally, like Bonnke, I often cannot fathom why God should not have chosen to heal Greg or others for whom it would have seemed humanly reasonable to do so. Much remains mysterious.

Can I suggest that we humbly pray for the sick, the cancerous, the dying, and not get discouraged. The decision to heal will always be His and His alone. It's not our agenda ultimately that matters. Don't be like doubting Thomas or the lady on the beach. Our job is to believe in Jesus, obey his commands, and benefit our friends, family or even ourselves by praying. We leave what happens to him.

Chapter Seventeen

HOW LONG HAVE I GOT?

Worship the LORD your God, and his blessing will be on your food and water. I will take away sickness from among you, and none will miscarry or be barren in your land. I will give you a full life span.[70]

As a doctor receiving my own diagnosis, the word "cancer" wasn't on its own at the forefront of my mind. Suspecting the worst, the bigger question for me was "How bad?" Not greatly cheered to learn of its friend the lymph node, I was glad to hear that the tumour had not progressed deeply into the bowel wall, and that no further spread had been detected. If information is power, my advisors and I now had the wherewithal to plan a strategy based on my likely chances of survival.

For many years, I have prayed for a long life. I don't think that is unduly selfish as there is so much I hope to do on this earth and not just for myself. A hundred will do nicely, Lord, and nothing so far has shifted my hope in living almost as long again as I have racked up so far. And I suspect I am not alone here. Cancer is a shocking diagnosis but why not take God at His word and worshipfully ask Him for a full life span? I am asking, and look forward to finding out how long that proves to be! But passionate though I am about personal longevity, there is arguably a greater question to be faced.

The medical profession, along with teachers, sanitation experts and others, have succeeded greatly in lengthening the average Western life. A hundred is by no means an unreasonable proposition for one born today, but the achievement comes at a price. For many years, my wife and I have been distressed by the success of pills in prolonging lives often at the expense of quality. As GPs we are leant on heavily to reach targets for BPs, sugars, cholesterols and the like, but as we do so, some miserably lengthened lives peer back at us. Sometimes, like all doctors, we rebel and make a decision based on the patient's overall best interests, rather than on numbers. It is called kindness and wisdom, but the pressure to conform and treat all to avoid any accusation of slack doctoring is always there.

Heather is vocal on the subject. In her mind, quality always trumps quantity and such a fate must not befall her. Maybe I am greedy because given the choice I would go for both, but if I could only have one and not the other, I too would plump for quality. For the big question should not be *"How long will I live?"* but *"How well can I live?"* And when cancer has taken a hold and puts quantity at real risk, the quality that perhaps we had taken for granted before must now assume centre stage.

Two disciples were walking to a village called Emmaus. Jesus had been resurrected but not all who would see him alive had done so by this point. Appearing alongside them, he feigned lack of knowledge of what was going on, in order to reveal their thoughts before explaining the Scriptures concerning himself. Urged to stay, for the day was almost over...

When he was at the table with them, he took bread, gave thanks, broke it and began to give it to them. Then their eyes were opened and they recognised him, and he disappeared from their sight. They asked each other, "Were not our hearts burning within us while he talked with us on the road and opened the Scriptures to us?"

They got up and returned at once to Jerusalem. There they found the Eleven and those with them, assembled together and saying, "It is true! The Lord has risen and has appeared to Simon." [71]

Meeting Jesus face-to-face now re-ordered the disciples' lives and priorities. No longer afraid and downcast, they were ready for whatever God had in store for them next. Many of their lives would be short, and John's would conclude in exile, but what they achieved in spreading the gospel was of enormous benefit to mankind.

This might not have been how they would have planned things! Given the choice, they might have wanted a few more years learning on the job with Jesus physically still there to correct any mistake – perhaps a gentle spiritual apprenticeship somewhere not too challenging, as they continued to learn the ropes! God had a different plan. Thrown into battle, but with the presence of the Holy Spirit, their work was about to be extended dramatically, beyond anything they could have imagined. The disciples would find themselves moving into a battle about which Jesus had given them warning and equipping, but much was still to unfold.

The cancer sufferer is stepping into quite uncharted waters. Christian believers can be assured of the presence of the living God as we face the future with the Holy Spirit guiding, indwelling, filling us as we ask in faith. Although we can't control the length of our lives, we can have some influence on their quality.

How? I would suggest first that "same old, same old" no longer applies. Life is *not* the same and, even if one recovers fully, it never will be. A brush with mortality not only closes doors in life – whether physical, financial or social – but opens doors in our minds that were shut or merely vaguely ajar before the tumult.

Some years ago, my younger sister nearly drowned in a canoeing accident. Tipped out of the boat, she was unable to free herself as her coat became caught on the edge, and she was rescued only just in time. Back on shore, she needed her lungs pumped and was fortunate to get away with just a patch of pneumonia. Some time afterwards, I took her for a curry, as brothers do, and plucked up courage. My sister has never shown any interest in God, but as we chatted, I asked whether she had thanked Him for her survival. To my amazement, she had; no overt belief, but a time of crisis had released something that had lain dormant all these years – something that just needed a good enough reason to see the light of day.

Sadly, her experience was short-lived. Returning to normality, the disastrous episode has been consigned to history. But cancer, in one sense, is forever. Even if in remission or potentially cured, at the back of one's mind is the thought that one day the beggar might just return. But on the plus side, our brush with mortality can really sharpen our minds. Firstly, *What can I still do?* Next, *OK, this is what's possible but what's really vital in the years, months, weeks I have left?* With changed priorities, all of these self-interrogations can be summed up in a wonderful question posed at the end of the Christian Alpha course: *"How can I make the most of the rest of my life?"* Naturally, such questions apply to time spent with family and friends as well as that required in organising our work and other aspects of life. But with time possibly short and priorities shifting, this re-prioritisation should take in the day to day and the eternal. Jesus has always been concerned with both.

Appearing again to his disciples after Calvary, he said, ***"Peace be with you."***

They were startled and frightened, thinking they saw a ghost. He said to them, "Why are you troubled, and why do doubts rise in your minds? Look at my hands and my feet. It is I myself! Touch me and see; a ghost does not have flesh and bones, as you see I have."

When he had said this, he showed them his hands and feet. And while they still did not believe it because of joy and amazement, he asked them, "Do you have anything here to eat?" They gave him a piece of broiled fish, and he took it and ate it in their presence.[72]

The disciples were startled, but Jesus brought them back to earth. Quite deliberately he reassured them with his wounds before grounding them in the mundane by eating fish. Only then could he teach them what they needed to know. And there is much that we need to know. Time may be short and big questions won't go away. But as we explore them, let's not forget that God is still very much with us in the common, everyday aspects of life. Like food and health.

One thing that strikes me about the passage is why did Jesus bother to eat? It wasn't that he was hungry; the emphasis doesn't support that, and all that was really needed was to prove his mastery over death by showing them his hands and feet. Just time then for a last blessing before he ascended. Equally, why does God heal some with cancer and lengthen the lives of others, when all that matters at the end of time is for them to believe in Him?

Well, healing is not a *right*, something we *deserve*, it is a *gift*, revealing something about the Kingdom. What we can see is that Jesus got involved in our world, even with all the pain and suffering it had caused him, and was not above eating fish to help the disciples and us to see something vital. His doing so, above all, revealed that his resurrection really was the resurrection of the body, not just a ghostly apparition.

Our lives matter to God. If the very hairs on our head are

known to Him, how much more the manner in which we live our lives. Of course, the way we do so depends on our beliefs and these may be under considerable challenge as events unfold. I remember discussing life's big questions with a man in his early sixties who had just recovered from a heart attack. *"Makes you think, doesn't it"*, I ventured at the end, and he agreed. How could it fail to, when his prospects in cardiac ITU weren't good, and everything he had held dear was under threat. His life could not remain the same, and not just physically. But I would argue that unless he resolved to explore the ultimate meaning of life, and really seek God through Jesus – who, as he claimed, is the Way, the Truth and the Life – that patient would miss out on the opportunity which a near death experience had provided. We will explore this more in the next chapter.

Chapter Eighteen

WHY DON'T I JUST END IT ALL?

"You shall not murder." [73]

One of the greatest ethical challenges doctors face at present is whether to get involved in assisted suicide. During a home visit recently I was asked whether I could "help a patient out" in this way. Responding that I would rather improve her pain relief, and that euthanising her was incompatible with both the Hippocratic oath and my Christian faith, I did my best in difficult circumstances; but her statement that she had had enough reflects an attitude that is becoming increasingly prominent in Western society. With or without my help, she saw it as *her* choice and was not concerned that suicide, whether assisted or not, acts deliberately to kill a person and therefore is a form of murder.

Cancer patients may similarly be at a low ebb. A disastrous diagnosis and life as good as over, except that it isn't, with much nastiness ahead culminating in an unpleasant end – what is there to live for? Why not end it all and save everybody a great deal of trouble? After all, others with chronic diseases occasionally assert their legal "rights" over their bodies and go down this route, ending in premature death either at their own hands or those of their supporters.

Why should cancer be any different?

Firstly, I would agree that cancer is not inherently different from any other chronic disease likely to shorten the life of a patient, so my comments apply equally to all patients faced with life-threatening conditions. Some of these can be extremely unpleasant and prolonged, and I am sympathetic to the plight of those for whom life seems intolerable. Many argue that we would not prolong the life of an animal in similar circumstances, and they are right: my beloved but elderly Labrador is deteriorating, and the time may come when her quality of life is so poor that we ask the vet to do the necessary. But humans are different; only we are made in God's image and are viewed by Him in a different light from all other creatures. Special to God, we are also part of a bigger picture.

There is a wonderful DVD entitled *Indescribable*, in which the evangelist Louie Giglio attempts to describe the universe in terms of numbers. Showing the stars in their billions, and reflecting on the millions of light years each is distant from us, he reveals the magnitude of God's work.[74] And a Psalm affirms:

> *When I consider your heavens,*
> *the work of your fingers,*
> *the moon and the stars,*
> *which you have set in place,*
> *what is man that you are mindful of him,*
> *the son of man that you care for him?*[75]

That brief statement is enough to redirect our thoughts to God; we too are the work of His hands though we are ridiculously tiny in comparison with even the smallest star. The psalmist continues:

You made him a little lower than the heavenly beings
and crowned him with glory and honour.
You made him ruler over the works of your hands;
You put everything under his feet:
all flocks and herds,
and the beasts of the field,
the birds of the air,
and the fish of the sea,
all that swim the paths of the seas.
O LORD, our Lord,
how majestic is your name in all the earth![76]

We may be tiny but we are special and truly important to God. No matter what our physical or mental state, no matter how awful we may view our situation as being, He still cares for us and regards us as in charge of the whole earth; but don't ignore the last line. Provided with everything and given a big job to boot, we respond in praise, at least that is how it is intended. A slightly corny phrase has entered the Christian lexicon in recent years, but it is worthy of repetition. An "attitude of gratitude" enables us to spend whatever time we are given on this earth positively, appreciatively and expectantly in relation to the future. Many people now expect to live much longer on this earth than three score years and ten, but whether a cancer patient dies in his mid-teens from an aggressive sarcoma, or eventually succumbs from prostatic secondaries in his late eighties, ultimately matters little. Our time on earth is still so limited. But our brief lives here have vast significance spiritually.

The author of Ecclesiastes was convinced that only in God did life have true meaning and pleasure.

He has made everything beautiful in its time. He has also set eternity in the hearts of men; yet they cannot fathom what God has done from beginning to end. I know there is nothing better for men than to be happy and do good while they live. That everyone may eat and drink, and find satisfaction in all his toil – this is the gift of God. I know that everything God does will endure for ever; nothing can be added to it and nothing taken from it. God does it so that men will revere him.[77]

We can enjoy a beautiful world because God provides, and as we respond in praise our hearts get a glimpse of eternity. It is a simple, revealed truth, but the author of these blessings is often forgotten, with an attitude of gratitude seen merely as being an optional extra for those who are religiously inclined. Just as our children often fail to appreciate what we give them, we may fail to appreciate the author of all good gifts. This then leads to what has been given becoming devalued. A dangerous slope … leading to euthanasia, suicide and assisted suicide.

Life is a great gift from God. Adam was formed from the dust of the ground, and God, *... breathed into his nostrils the breath of life, and the man became a living being.*[78]

Furthermore, the Bible is clear that God has the right to give and take away. When Satan first afflicted Job, killing his children, his servants and his livestock, *... he fell to the ground in worship and said:*

> *"Naked I came from my mother's womb,*
> *and naked I shall depart.*
> *The LORD gave and the LORD has taken away;*
> *may the name of the LORD be praised."*

There won't be many families, with or without cancer, who suffer to the extent that Job's did, yet the passage continued by stating: *In all this, Job did not sin by charging God with wrongdoing.*[79]

The main reason I believe that people consider suicide or assisted suicide in terminal illness like cancer is that they have no concept of God. They view life as simply a basic human right to be exercised as we see fit, rather than a gift from God for which we are grateful and which is given for the length of His choosing. A second reason is that, unlike Job, they lose faith in God or charge Him with wrongdoing. *"This isn't fair, it's not right, in fact it's simply unreasonable for me to get cancer in the prime of life when my friends are OK."* Some people think of cancer as being God's fault, and so, in their minds, He forfeits the right to have a say in their continued existence. This idea is deeply flawed.

We have already seen that sickness and death were never God's intention and only entered our world after mankind's disobedience resulted in the Fall. Secondly, God not only gives us life but maintains it for our span on earth, with eternity ahead and beckoning. An eternity in which cancer is absent. Pain is absent. Only good stuff will be found in God's new heaven and earth. There will be nothing substandard or unwelcome. When Jesus comes again, all that is evil will be destroyed and that's that! What all this means for anyone considering doing away with themselves is immense.

Looking back over my life – and anyone who knows me will concur – there are times when I haven't done well. Events which cause me anguish even today sometimes register and I am downcast, hardly able to believe twenty to thirty years later that I could be capable of such idiocy. But when I returned to the Lord half a lifetime ago, forgiveness was on the table. And I took it, so desperate was I not to carry around my failures, the hurts I had caused, any longer. And as (for a second time) I resolved to follow Jesus, I knew that any sins could be laid at the foot of the Cross.

Believers know that we are already living 'in Christ' and that eternal life continues beyond this world, so we really do have something extraordinary to look forward to – an eternal future with God, in the company of other believers – a future which has been set out in advance, for Jesus promised that he would prepare a place which will be ready for us when the time comes. The Bible also describes that future as being like a wedding feast, with continual rejoicing and with no pain, no suffering and, crucially, no sin.

Here is the problem: "mercy killing" and suicide, whether assisted or not, are forms of murder. As a person approaches the end of their time here, the temptation to do away with oneself, whether at one's own hand or through the hands of others, may be strong. Friends and family may support your decision and even some doctors may concur and be prepared to help, but having numbers on your side doesn't alter the basic premise one jot. Murder is specifically prohibited by God, and like all other sins, acts to separate us from our perfect Father. Furthermore, not only does it show profound disregard for one of God's greatest gifts, life itself, but its very finality provides no subsequent opportunity for repentance.

It is important for those tempted in this way to remember that the act can affect or implicate others, who may have approved such deliberate ending of life or may become accessories to it. Not only are we to avoid sin in ourselves, we also have a duty not to lead others into sin.

Don't be tempted! God made you and will take you when He is ready. He is keeping you where you are for a purpose. Every day provides opportunities to do something for God: witnessing for Him, praying, simply depending on Him, trusting in Him. Seek the very best palliative care for relief of pain for yourself or your dying loved one, and continue to seek and enjoy a closer relationship with Jesus – even at the very moment when God takes you from this world.

Chapter Nineteen

I'M NO HYPOCRITE

Meanwhile, Saul was still breathing out murderous threats against the Lord's disciples. He went to the high priest and asked him for letters to the synagogues in Damascus, so that if he found any there who belonged to the Way, whether men or women, he might take them as prisoners to Jerusalem. As he neared Damascus on his journey, suddenly a light from heaven flashed around him. He fell to the ground and heard a voice say to him, "Saul, Saul, why do you persecute me?"

"Who are you, Lord?" Saul asked.

"I am Jesus, whom you are persecuting," he replied, "Now get up and go into the city, and you will be told what you must do." [80]

Saul had a clear path in life. A traditional Jew, born well and educated in exemplary fashion, he had become very powerful and was using his position to do what he thought most important in life – wiping out this new sect of Christians, who he saw as a threat to his religious heritage. On his way to cause further destruction, he encountered a rather more powerful force than himself: Jesus. Blinded for three days and not eating or drinking, he was led by his fellow travellers into Damascus, where he met a man named Ananias, whom God had primed in advance to provide help. Told in a vision what must take place, Ananias, was not only amazed but also naturally somewhat reluctant. Only too aware of Saul's threat to Christians, he needed God's reassurance that Saul was a changed man and that he had been chosen to reach out to the Gentiles and the people of Israel. Placing his hands on Saul, the scales fell from his eyes and he could see again. The Bible goes on to say that he got up, was baptised, took food and regained his strength.

For Saul, this was crisis time. For a proud man, falling to the ground and then temporarily going blind must have been bad enough, but to learn that spiritually he had got things completely wrong and was persecuting the very Lord over all must have shaken him to the core. He did what he was told, regained his sight and then had a choice to make. Should he ignore what had taken place, massive though it had been, and continue his previous life, or wise-up and follow the path Jesus had mapped out for him? We know that he chose the second option, one that would endear him to Christians but not to those to whom he had previously belonged. Changing his allegiance would not only make him new friends but also new enemies.

Becoming a Christian inevitably involves a change of allegiance. With only two options available and no middle way, the change may not be easy. Some may feel that switching from a lifetime of faithlessness to one in which they place their faith and trust in God is not possible, for a couple of reasons. Firstly, it would imply that, like Saul, their lives up to that point had followed the wrong path, and had been foolish, even pointless. This can be seriously upsetting for the ego! Secondly, and perhaps even more potently, they may feel that a sea-change in philosophy is somehow "hypocritical" – that in committing themselves to Jesus they are being disloyal to something or someone in the past. As a result, a misplaced sense of being deceitful or duplicitous may emerge, delaying or even preventing the most important commitment any of us could ever make. This needs some fleshing out.

Heather has always loved compiling scrapbooks. From childhood to the present day, her photos are a record of the lives of those she has loved, whether school friends, family or even myself. In time, the best prints from the Canaries at Easter will join their predecessors, although not all the cacti I snapped in profusion I suspect will make the final cut! Photos are precious – one of the few things you might rush back into a burning house to retrieve. And for those who have lost a loved one, they are all the more cherished.

Memories are triggered by photos. A picture of my Dutch uncle, who died two years before I wrote this book, is on my study desk. I had last seen him alive in the summer. We chatted then about practical affairs – whether he should continue with regular blood transfusions for marrow failure, for he was of a mind not to – but also concerning spiritual matters. Jan was an old man, who in his physical weakness was looking forward to heaven. Relaxed about what lay ahead, at his funeral his faith was remembered, as members of a church that he had set up in Eindhoven spoke about him.

In visiting other old people, this time in a professional capacity, they will often refer to their lost spouse pictured alongside them. An elderly lady might suddenly exclaim, *"If only Jim was here"*; or, *"When my husband was alive...."* Memories of better times, tinged with regret for what has been lost, and usually with a determination that their relationship will always remain the same, husband and wife, together forever. And I smile, aware increasingly that this will happen to Heather or me one day, and not necessarily at that old lady's great age. But if time allows and we chat further, this sense of stability, of nothing changing, of sepia-tinged memories cast in stone, can have a sinister side.

My uncle Jan knew where he was going. His faith was secure, his trust in Jesus plain. Put another way, no-one had a hold on him. Family members might exert influence, especially as his physical powers faded, but the essential motivation within was subject to no man. He had made his decision based on the evidence, and no-one could take that from him. But others as they grow old can be so dominated by the past, by what "Jim" would have wanted, that they are in grave danger of losing out in the present and the future. Let me explain.

One of the devil's nastiest ploys is to persuade non-believers that they will be together after death. Deceived into believing that the God revealed in the Bible does not exist, and that sin, judgement, heaven and hell are not real, the surviving spouse waits to enter his or her grave alongside the lost partner, supposedly reunited after an unhappy interlude. And Satan will be laughing, because he knows full well that this scenario is impossible. With his own future in the fiery pit at the end of time confirmed, he intends to take as many of us with him as possible. What he doesn't want is for someone to have the courage to buck the trend and believe in Jesus Christ alone. And the influence of loved relatives can be most unhelpful.

Picture the scene. An old widow looks at her dead husband's photo and longs to be with him again. How natural, nothing wrong there. Or is there? He was a lifelong atheist, no interest in the God whom one day he will meet and bow before. And not wanting to rock the boat, his widow, who had been brought up in a Christian family but who had laid her faith aside at marriage, has lived a life essentially of faithlessness. A doctor visits and suggests that as time may be shortening, she reconsider her faith. *"But how can I?"*, she replies? *"It would be disloyal to Jim. I wouldn't want to go to heaven if he was in the other place and anyway, after a lifetime away, wouldn't it be hypocritical?"*

That widow, has expressed a view which is all too common. Her entire future, her spiritual destiny is wholly subservient to her desire to be with Jim forever. But how can they be? My biblical understanding of hell implies a place where God and goodness are entirely absent, replaced instead by ongoing and unrelenting woe. Within such a setting, how on earth – or how, in hell – does she expect to be holding hands with Jim? It is utterly illogical, fanciful and unrealistic. Bursting this bubble brings me back to cancer.

As has been seen already, cancer is not only a massive blow but a massive opportunity. Life is no longer the same, and pretending that it is, or that nothing can ever change, is illusory. Cancer may be the thing which triggers refocusing and new priorities, but only if we allow ourselves to change. Repentance and a living faith in God through Jesus is the best thing that can happen to a person. So why might such a declaration of faith fill either the patient or their family and friends with alarm? I think there are two main reasons.

The first is that in some way the new believer is not being "true to himself". His or her old life "philosophy" has been swept away, and a shift in allegiance from oneself to God is not always seen in a positive light by others. The person involved is most definitely not the same as before; the Bible talks about becoming a "new creation", and in coming to terms with this, the family and friends may use unflattering terms including "hypocrite" to describe the change in the man or woman they thought they knew.

The second reason is intimately linked to this. As severe illness has stripped away old certainties and caused the cancer patient to reflect on eternity, those close to him or her are confronted with their own positions. Where are they in relation to God, and what would happen if they became ill or died suddenly and unexpectedly? Change in the patient affects those around him or her, and not just in material terms. The patient's helpers, too, have the opportunity to reflect on what is going on and make changes in their own lives, before it is too late.

So does coming to faith makes someone a hypocrite? Hardly! It is the best possible thing in life, and it may be serious illness that brings someone to an awareness of their own mortality (which is not to say that the disease is good). Don't persuade yourself otherwise. And if that patient is you, and you are wondering what your husband or wife would say, or how your friends would take such a momentous decision, remember this: your whole future is at stake, not anyone else's. And your destiny is worked out only between you and God. Don't be like the widow who spent a lifetime fearing another's opinion of her. The Bible tells us clearly that the only one worth fearing is God, for He alone holds the keys to eternal life. His opinion matters hugely, others not at all. And know this: no matter how long your conversion has been in coming, it is just what God's been waiting for; and as the party begins in heaven, you may sense (and will one day know) that the angels are celebrating the wisest decision you could ever have made.

Chapter Twenty

I'M STILL NOT SURE

And without faith it is impossible to please God, because anyone who comes to him must believe that he exists and that he rewards those who earnestly seek him.[81]

Cancer specialises in raising doubts. Not just questions like *How long might I live?*, but genuine vacillation and wavering from one extreme to another. Hard on the heels of *I'm going to be healed* might be, *But how can you be so sure?* Or, alternatively, *Yippee, the scans are clear*, but *What if they've missed something?* Summed up by, *I trust my doctor implicitly, but....* Persistent doubts indicate a deeper problem. Recently, Heather mentioned a patient whose back pain was almost certainly linked to a collapsed vertebra. Seeing the patient twice for the same problem, the message clearly had not got through as she sought a second opinion in Casualty, only to be told the same thing after an X-ray confirmed the diagnosis.

Often, when folks have trouble accepting a diagnosis, it is not just that they doubt the messenger but that they don't like the message. They are looking for something else, although it is not always clear what. The lady on the beach had constructed a highly complex and illogical storyline through a series of mental gymnastics, rather than accept the simplicity of what God has laid down as truth. This is the kernel of the issue: do we accept God's version of events, or proudly make up our own, and through chronic indecision simply sit on the fence?

When my car misbehaves, I trust my mechanic to mend it safely. Similarly, when my body let me down, I was happy to rely on the surgeons and oncologists locally to treat me. Without that tyre being replaced or tumour being removed, my life would be at risk and so I am happy to take the expert's advice. "Ask the right person the right question and you are liable to get the right answer" has always been my policy. Most of us would agree that expertise in different areas of life is handy, but funny how the argument can be side-tracked in relation to faith.

The Bible tells us that God not only made us in His own image, but implants faith within us as a gift. All His gifts are good but our faith is particularly important to Him, for, *...without faith it is impossible to please God....*[82] Only too aware of our human tendency to doubt, God sent His only Son to live and die and be raised from the dead for us. Jesus showed us the way to the Father. We now have a great deal of consistent proof. Creation must have a Creator, the resurrected and perfect Jesus surely was, as he claimed, divine, and the influence of his people over the last 2,000 years testifies to the effect of lives changed by him. More than enough evidence to accept, should we choose to do so. And therein lies the crunch.

Many people have said to me, *I wish I could have your faith.* And I reply that they can, but only if they are willing to *seek* God. At a party recently, a woman asked me how I could be so sure. Receiving the same answer, she said she truly wanted to know more about God. I believed her and made a few suggestions, all along the line of "Seek and you will find." The difference in her was that she not only posed the question but desperately wanted the answer.

Because our faith in Jesus Christ is precious, its absence leads to a void in our relationship with God. He rewards the faithful further: *... For the eyes of the LORD range throughout the earth to strengthen those whose hearts are fully committed to him.*[83] Herein lies God's *modus operandi*: Believe and trust in my Son, Jesus, and I will strengthen you. Faith has consequences as we have seen throughout this book – and, as we take a first hesitant step, God helps our faith to grow.

But one significant question remains. *What happens if I simply don't believe in Him? Can't believe in Him? You can't force me!* Impasse. Like a side road advertised by a no-entry sign, faith here is wrongly thought of as a dead end. But the God revealed in the Bible is a God of justice. That means He is scrupulously fair – fair enough to give everyone a chance to hear the gospel *and* the ability to respond. While I accept that for some the road to faith may be more difficult and tortuous than for others, the idea that faith is only open to a pre-selected few is not one I share. God desires that all should come to know Him, and the gospel as preached by the first apostles is simple enough for all to understand and respond to.

God has taken the initiative. We now need to respond to His call by repenting and believing in Jesus and obeying him for evermore. All of us have been given this opportunity. But many have walked away from their eternal destiny, choosing to ignore God's voice. Medically, hardening of the arteries can be dangerous. Spiritually, hardening of our hearts may be terminal. Cancer, that other big killer, may be alerting us to the eternal danger we are in. In doing so, malignancy may encourage our hardened hearts to soften towards God's voice. As He calls us, giving us an opportunity, no-one has an excuse, for every one of us can respond to Him.

Cancer is the great equaliser. No respecter of country or status, it is far-reaching, nasty and often fatal. But if it draws us towards God, one of our greatest enemies may even have done us a favour. At the end of this book about the ultimate disease, I now present the ultimate choice. Will we choose to repent and believe, or not? Will we accept that faith literally is the catalyst for more faith, or continue to sit on the fence, waiting for yet another scrap of evidence to come our way? Knowing that faith can cause us to live more healthily on this earth, and certainly leads to eternal life, will we accept the free gift or decline it, living life as we have always done on a path to ultimate destruction?

With cancer, time may be short. The same can be true spiritually, for Scripture warns us:

So, as the Holy Spirit says:

"Today, if you hear his voice,
do not harden your hearts as you did in the rebellion,
during the time of testing in the desert,
where your fathers tested and tried me
and for forty years saw what I did.
That is why I was angry with that generation,
and I said, 'Their hearts are always going astray,
and they have not known my ways.'
So I declared on oath in my anger,
'They shall never enter my rest.'"[84]

With life at a low ebb, we may never have a better opportunity to accept the free gift of faith. This may be our time, but the longer we resist God's gracious offer, the more our hearts become hardened. What applied in Moses' time to Pharaoh, the man more than any other described as having a hard heart, is just as true for us today. Faced with God's power, he had ample evidence with which to change tack and believe, but chose not to. How foolish we now know he was, and how many of his men died as a result.

Choosing to believe in Jesus is not merely adopting a philosophical position akin to aligning oneself to a particular football team or adopting a favourite colour. It is choosing life itself.

Another word from the apostle Paul. Very keen that none should miss out on what he himself had received, he said this:

As God's fellow-workers we urge you not to receive God's grace in vain. For He says,

"In the time of my favour I heard you,
and in the day of salvation I helped you."

And Paul continued, *I tell you, now is the time of God's favour, now is the day of salvation.*[85]

He knew there was no time to lose. Making a decision for God is both wise and urgent. There is so much to gain and nothing to lose, except that which is worthless anyway. I don't yet know exactly why God allowed me to get cancer. You probably feel similarly about your own tumour or that of people you love. But if my cancer or yours helps you come to a living faith in God, the suffering and distress will have been worth it, even though the disease itself is a bad thing and God's will is to heal.

If you are ready to follow Jesus as your Saviour and Lord, entrusting the rest of your life to him alone, I suggest praying a prayer like that on the next page.

Having done so, you will have entered his Kingdom as an infant Christian. Please see your local pastor who will then instruct you how to grow.

A Believer's Prayer – for those with Cancer

Dear God, for too long I have gone my own way. Now I'm ill with cancer, I recognise that I need your forgiveness for all my sin. Forgive me for relying on myself, and for failing to thank and worship you as Lord; for all the wrongdoing and all the hurts I have caused others through what I've done and what I've failed to do. Especially, forgive me for....

At this point, mention anything that particularly troubles your conscience or that God has said is wrong. You don't have to remember everything, for the Cross covers it all. As the Holy Spirit brings things to mind, just lay them before the Cross and repent, which means saying you're sorry with a determination to follow God's way from now on.

Thank you for sending your only Son Jesus, who died on the Cross to pay the price for all my sins. Jesus – thank you for dying for me; I now ask you to be my Saviour and my Lord.

Father, fill me with your Holy Spirit and enable me to tell others about your wonderful Son Jesus. And grant me enough time on this earth to do whatever you have planned for me. In his name and for his glory. *Amen.*

Lord God, in the name of Jesus, I ask you now to heal me.

POSTSCRIPT

Following diagnosis with rectal cancer in 2011, I underwent a year's treatment, involving surgery, radiotherapy and two separate regimes of chemotherapy. A year later, I was able to return to normal work as a family doctor (GP), but with three-monthly scans and regular endoscopies monitoring my situation. I am fully well now.

I give thanks to God for this healing, and I am grateful for considerable prayer from many sources. I also benefited from a prophetic word given to a Christian colleague before I had even declared my symptoms, stating that "this disease will not end in death".

Richard Scott

NOTES

1. Diamond, John, *C – Because Cowards get Cancer too...,* (Vermillion, 1998). Used by permission of the Random House Group Ltd. Permission also sought (for US rights) from Ed Victor Ltd.

2. Ashton, Mark (Rev), *On my Way to Heaven – Facing Death with Christ* (IO Publishing, 2010).

3. Judges 6:3–6

4. *Encyclopaedia Britannica* 1970, Vol. 4, pp. 769, 774.

5. American Cancer Society

6. 1 Samuel 17:4

7. Job 2:6

8. Job 42:17

9. My thanks to Dr. Rakesh Raman, Consultant Oncologist at QEQM Hospital, Margate, for providing me with computer-generated information about this theoretical patient.

10. I am grateful to the following organisations for their statistics published online: Cancer Research UK, World Cancer Research Fund, United Kingdom Association of Cancer Registries, British Journal of Cancer and American Cancer Society.

11. John 5:2–9

12. Hinn, Benny *The Anointing*, (Thomas Nelson, 1997), p. 95.

13. Koenig, McCullough and Larson *Handbook of Religion and Health*, 1st edition, (Oxford University Press, 2001)

14. Koenig, King and Carson *Handbook of Religion and Health*, 2nd edition, (Oxford University Press, 2012).

15. Philippians 4:6–7

16. 2 Kings 20:1–6

17. 2 Kings 18:5–7

18. I am indebted to the *Handbook of Religion and Health*, 2nd edition, *op. cit.* pp. 405-6 for providing this account.

19. Matthew 19:26

20. McAll, Graham (Dr.) *At a Given Moment – Faith Matters in Healthcare Encounters*, Christian Medical Fellowship, 2011), pp.168–9.

21. United States Cancer Statistics 2007, Incidence and Mortality. Thanks to the National Center for Chronic Disease Prevention and Health Promotion and the National Program of Cancer Registries.

22. *Op. cit. Handbook of Religion and Health*, 1st edition.

23. Acts 3:1–10

24. John 14:12–14

25. Wilson, Julian *Wigglesworth: the Complete Story*, (Authentic, 2002), ISBN 1–86024–237–5. Permission granted by Authentic Media.

26. Hibbert, Albert *Smith Wigglesworth: the Secret of his Power*, (Sovereign World, 1987), ISBN 1–85240–004–8. Permission granted by Harrison House.

27. Buckingham, Jamie *Daughter of Destiny: the only Authorized Biography of Kathryn Kuhlman*, (Bridge-Logos, rpt. 2008), ISBN 978–0–88270–784–6. Permission granted to use specified material by Bridge-Logos publishers.

28. Taken from *Living a Life of Fire: Reinhard Bonnke, an Autobiography*, (E-R Productions, 2009). ISBN 978–1–933106–81–6. Permission granted to publish these extracts from *Living a Life of Fire* granted by E-R Productions.

29. Cruz, Nicky *One Holy Fire*, (Hodder & Stoughton, 2007). ISBN 978–0–340–86187–5

30. Taken from *There is Always Enough* – detailing the ministries of Rolland and Heidi Baker. ISBN 978–1–85240–542–7. Reprinted by permission. *There is Always Enough*, Rolland and Heidi Baker, (copyright © Sovereign World Ltd, Lancaster, England, 2003. All rights reserved).

31. Johnson, Bill, *When Heaven Invades Earth* and *Supernatural Power of a Transformed Mind*, (jointly published by Authentic Media Ltd, 2011), ISBN 978–1–85078–952-9 Reproduced by permission of Destiny Image Publishers.

32. James 5:16

33. John 14:11–12

34. John 3:8

35. Lubbock, Margaret *Encounters with God*, copyright c/o Margaret Lubbock, 2009

36. 1 Chronicles 4:9–10

37. Reported in *Christianity* magazine, July 2012, p. 9

38. Director of Radiotherapy and Radiology in New Zealand, quoted in the Palmerston North Evening Standard, June 7th, 1973, and reproduced in *Fear no Evil*, by Canon David Watson, (Hodder & Stoughton, 1983), p. 161.

NOTES

39. Diamond, J *op. cit.*

40. Casson, James *"Dying - the greatest adventure of my life"- a young family doctor tells his story*, first pub. 1980; with the second section of the book entitled *My Cancer* by Peter Casson (his son), first pub. 1996 by the Christian Medical Fellowship, London

41. Drain, A. J. *"Code Red" – a young Christian surgeon finds Job helps him face death*, 2010, Christian Medical Fellowship

42. Watson, D *Fear no Evil* (Hodder and Stoughton, 1983).

43. Proverbs 12:25a

44. Luke 13:10–17

45. Luke 13:32–33

46. Luke 18:31–33

47. Luke 18:34

48. Mark 9:21–24

49. Luke 19:28–31

50. Luke 19:36–37

51. Luke 21:38

52. Matthew 26:31–35

53. Jeremiah 1:4–8; the call of Jeremiah

54. *Where is God when it Hurts?*, Rev. Dr. Rob Bewley, New Wine Magazine, Summer 2012, p44. This is material copyright New Wine Magazine, www.new-wine.org and used with permission

55. Luke 10:38–42

56. Luke 22:41–44

57. Jeremiah 29:11–14a

58. 1 Kings 19:9b–10

59. Luke 22:54–61

60. Matthew 27:46 (means, "My God, my God, why have you forsaken me?")

61. Exodus 14:29–31

62. Exodus 14:12–14

63. John 20:19–20

64. Psalm 46:1

65. Acts 7:59–60

66. Acts 7:56

67. John 20:24–29

68. Psalm 103:1–3

69. James 5:14–15a

70. Exodus 23:25–26

71. Luke 24:30–34
72. Luke 24:36–43
73. Exodus 20:13 – the Ten Commandments
74. *Indescribable*, Louis Giglio, 2009, ASIN B002EIJ8KO
75. Psalm 8:3–4
76. Psalm 8:5–9
77. Ecclesiastes 3:11–14
78. Genesis 2:7
79. Job 1:20–22
80. Acts 9:1–6
81. Hebrews 11:6
82. Hebrews 11:6
83. 2 Chronicles 16:9
84. Hebrews 3:7–11
85. 2 Corinthians 6:1–2

By the same author:

Christians in the Firing Line (Wilberforce, 2013)